The Island Plate II

More Recipes from The Honolulu Advertiser

Wanda A. Adams

Advertiser Food Editor

ISLAND HERITAGE™
PUBLISHING

Cover: 2008, Artwork by IHP Archive.

Food styling: Iwa Bush

Photos:
  Pages 1, 5, 6, 12, 16, 17, 18, 19, 21, 22, 23, 26, 32, 33, 35, 36, 39, 41, 42, 44, 46, 47, 50, 55, 58, 59, 60,
      62, 63, 64, 66, 69, 73, 74, 77, 78, 81, 82, 83, 84, 90, 91, 94, 97, 98, 101, 102, 106, 109, 110, 111,
      113, 123, 124, 127, 129, 131, 132, 134: Roméo S. Collado.
  Page 1: exotic beverage ©iStockphoto.com/Lise Gagne, umbrella ©iStockphoto.com/KMITU
  Page 4: IHP
  Page 8: lime ©iStockphoto.com/AchimPrill
  Page 10, 105: eggs ©iStockphoto.com/Branislav Senic
  Page 11, 64: parsley ©iStockphoto.com/Floortje
  Page 13, 57: green onions ©iStockphoto.com/P_Wei
  Page 15: Bruce Asato, Oct. 30, 2006
  Page 24: food ingredients ©iStockphoto.com/MKucova
  Page 25: Richard Ambo, April 12, 2006
  Page 28: peanuts ©iStockphoto.com/Matej Michelizza
  Page 30: Jeff Widener, Jan. 27, 2005
  Page 42: ginger ©iStockphoto.com/Yekaterina Choupova
  Page 43: soybeans ©iStockphoto.com/Steve Dibblee
  Page 49: peas ©iStockphoto.com/gabrieldome
  Page 52, 133: onions ©iStockphoto.com/Angel Rodriguez
  Page 56, 87: potatoes ©iStockphoto.com/Lakov Kalinin
  Page 61: macadamia ©iStockphoto.com/Georg Hergenhan
  Page 65: bok choy ©iStockphoto.com/Ivana Starcevic
  Page 70: Deborah Booker, July 18, 2007
  Page 71, 89: tomatoes ©iStockphoto.com/Kolan
  Page 96: coconut ©iStockphoto.com/Michael Valdez
  Page 104: blueberries ©iStockphoto.com/Nikola Bilic
  Page 115: raspberries ©iStockphoto.com/Pedro Tavares
  Page 116: baking ingredients ©iStockphoto.com/Lowell Sannes
  Page 130: walnuts ©iStockphoto.com/Elena Elisseeva
  Pages 142: Greg Yamamoto, The Honolulu Advertiser

Published by

ISLAND HERITAGE™
P U B L I S H I N G
A DIVISION OF THE MADDEN CORPORATION

94-411 KŌʻAKI STREET, WAIPAHU, HAWAIʻI 96797-2806
Orders: (800) 468-2800 • Information: (808) 564-8800
Fax: (808) 564-8877
islandheritage.com

ISBN#: 1-59700-611-4
First Edition, Second Printing - 2009

contents

Dedication

To all my cooking mothers: Grandma Ida,
Mom Addie, Godmother Cyrilla,
Mom-in-law Grayce, Aloha, Signe,
Jane, Nancy, Hildreth, Janice,
Harriet, and all the others who
have nurtured me in their kitchens.
You have afforded me lifelong pleasure
and an unending challenge.

Acknowledgments

Marylene Chun, deputy tester and the culinary
"therapist" who kept me sane

Newsroom colleagues, particularly Elizabeth Kieszkowski,
Gregory Yamamoto, and David Yamada

The capable and cooperative team at the Madden Corporation/Island Heritage

Bakers extraordinaire Shirley Higa and Sugar Rush by Frances,
(www.sugarrushhi.com) for key assists during food photography

Taster-in-chief "Sonny" Koonce, who lost his wife to the
computer and the kitchen for a couple of months.
"If I had to live without you, what kind of life would that be?"

— Wanda Adelaide Adams, Kapālama, March 2006
Aloha kākou!

Introduction

Ever since *The Island Plate: 150 Years of Recipes and Food Lore from The Honolulu Advertiser* appeared and promptly sold out in its first edition in 2005, people have been asking "When's the next one?" This question made me want to lie down in a dark room and suck my thumb. But here it is, thanks to *Advertiser* president and publisher Lee Webber, editor Mark Platte, and events manager Darilyn Fernandez; to Dale and Lynne Madden and the team at the Madden Corporation/Island Heritage; and to my husband's unending patience (and willingness to eat anything).

This is less a history and more a cookbook than *The Island Plate*, but I have placed every dish in context and told its story so far as I knew it. And you will find some amusing asides from the *Advertiser* files for those who enjoy reading cookbooks more than cooking from them.

Once again: Fill your plate with *aloha*!

Send your feedback to me, Wanda Adams, at wadams@honoluluadvertiser.com; (808) 535-2412.

Where to find ingredients if you don't live in Hawai'i

Wherever you see the symbol , we're telling you that you'll find this ingredient in a well-stocked Asian grocery or online.

Online sources for Asian foods include Asian Food Grocer (www.asianfoodgrocer.com) or toll-free, 1 (888) 482-2742; Koa Mart (www.koamart.com); and Yollie's Oriental Market & Gift Shop (www.yollieoriental.com).

The Hawai'i Store (www.dahawaiistore.com) or (808) 841-8829 and SureSave Supermarket (www.suresave.com) are good resources for Hawaiian food and favorite Island products.

Things change fast on the Internet, so try plugging an ingredient or ethnicity into a search engine with the words "food" and "mail order" to find other sources.

Wherever possible, we've suggested substitutions. For example, canned peaches can be used wherever fresh mango is called for.

CHAPTER 1

Da Kine

DRINKS AND DRESSINGS;
PRESERVES AND PICKLES;
SNACKS, BREADS, AND ODDITIES

D a kine – it's what we say when we can't quite think of the word we need.
Funny thing: two Islanders always understand each other, even without nouns. "Hand me da kine." "Wheah da kine stay?" "You get any da kine?"

So you, dear reader, will understand that this is a mixed-up chop suey of a chapter — anything that's not a pūpū or potluck dish, an entrée, a salad, soup, or side dish, or a dessert has been included here.

You know, da kine.

Drinks

Juice-flavored iced teas (a.k.a. plantation iced tea) are an Island staple, though served more often in restaurants than at home now. To make this old-time recipe more contemporary, use green tea. And if someone wants to add a splash of rum, *'a'ole pilikia* (no problem)!

Hawaiian Iced Tea | Appeared Sept. 12, 1957

6 ounces chilled unsweetened iced tea
1 tablespoon simple syrup (recipe follows)
3 tablespoons pineapple juice
2 teaspoons fresh lime juice
Dash of bitters
Crushed ice
Lime wedge

Combine liquid ingredients in a cocktail shaker and mix ❖ Fill a tall glass half with crushed ice and half with mixed liquids ❖ Garnish with lime wedge.

❖ *Serves 1.*

Simple Syrup

Simple syrup is used in everything from Southern-style "sweet tea" to a gin fizz. This cooked sugar mixture is useful for sweetening cold mixtures without a grainy texture.

2   cups sugar
1   cup water

In a saucepan, combine sugar and water ✤ Bring to a boil; stir and boil gently 5 minutes ✤ Keeps for 6 months in the refrigerator.

✤ *Makes 2 cups.*

— from *101 Great Tropical Drinks* by Cheryl Chee Tsutsumi (Island Heritage)

Columnist Maili Yardley offered a sketchy recipe for an unusual punch using fresh or frozen fruit juices. If you're lucky enough to have a Surinam cherry tree nearby, and access to passion fruit, this sprightly punch will knock you out. Use commercial sweetened guava and pineapple juices but make fresh, unsweetened Surinam cherry and passion fruit juices, since these are rarely commercially available. If you can't find Surinam cherries or passion fruit juice, substitute with pomegranate juice.

A Hawaiian Punch | Appeared Sept. 24, 1989

1   cup guava juice
½   cup unsweetened Surinam cherry juice (see Note)
½   cup unsweetened passion fruit juice (see Note)
1   cup pineapple juice
½-1 cup simple syrup (see above)
Ice

In pitcher or punch bowl, combine juices ✤ Add ½ cup simple syrup; taste and add more sugar syrup, if needed ✤ Chill completely ✤ Serve iced.

✤ *Serves 4.*

Note: To juice Surinam cherries: Wash and stem 2 pounds Surinam cherries; place in saucepan with water barely to cover; mash and simmer until soft. Place in muslin jelly bag or several layers of cheesecloth, tie up and allow to drip. Discard solids.

To juice passion fruit:
Cut 1 dozen passion fruit in half and place in muslin jelly bag or several layers of cheesecloth; squeeze to express juice. Discard solids.

What's a Surinam cherry?

These puckery ribbed fruit (*Eugenia uniflora*) resemble miniature pumpkins, in colors ranging from crimson to tangerine. Island kids conduct "cherry wars," firing the overripe fruit that, when thrown vigorously, hit the target with a satisfying splat, creating dramatic stains to their mothers' despair. The cherry is getting a lot of attention, too: the second-season winner of Bravo's *Top Chef*, Ilan Hall, used Surinam cherries in a sorbet that helped land him the title here in Hawai'i and the University of Hawai'i is studying the fruit's commercial potential (the juice is big business in Brazil). Good to know: the cherries are, as we say in pidgin, "Sow-ah, sow-ah, sow-ah" (sour, sour, sour)! Mix one part juice or pulp to one part sugar in drinks and preserves.

Dressings and Sauces

The food processor has made making mayonnaise from scratch ridiculously easy. My preference: homemade mayonnaise for cold sauces and sophisticated salads; commercial mayonnaise for potato-mac salads and sandwiches. Using pasteurized eggs can reduce the danger of illness from tainted raw eggs. Mayonnaise requires a bland oil (vegetable oil, canola, or grape seed); olive oil has too pronounced a flavor.

Homemade Mayonnaise | Appeared May 6, 1943

- 1 teaspoon salt
- 1 teaspoon sugar
- 1 teaspoon dry mustard
- 1 egg
- 1 egg yolk
- 2 tablespoons lemon juice or vinegar, or to taste
- 1 $\frac{1}{2}$-2 cups vegetable oil

In the bowl of a food processor fitted with a metal blade, combine salt, sugar, mustard, whole egg, egg yolk, and lemon juice or vinegar ❖ Process 15 seconds, just to combine ❖ With the processor running constantly, start by adding a few drops oil at a time and work up to a steady, thin stream ❖ The mayonnaise is done when the mixture increases in volume and takes on the look and texture of mayonnaise ❖ Correct seasonings to taste.

❖ *Makes about 2 cups.*

On most tables, tartar sauce means nothing more than a little chopped onion and sweet pickle relish stirred into mayonnaise. But in 1950, Advertiser editors claimed that the original, spelled tartare sauce, was made with olive oil and the pounded yolks of hard-boiled eggs. They went on, however, to offer a more conventional version. Serve with lean grilled or fried fish.

Tartar Sauce | Appeared Feb. 9, 1950

1   cup Homemade Mayonnaise (see page 10)
2   teaspoons vinegar
2   tablespoons chopped sweet pickle
2   teaspoons finely minced chives
1   tablespoon finely minced parsley
2   teaspoons finely chopped capers

Few drops onion juice (see Note)
2   tablespoons chopped green olives
      (optional)
Freshly ground pepper
Salt, if needed

Place mayonnaise in a medium bowl and stir in remaining ingredients except pepper and salt ❖ Cover, chill, and allow to season a few hours or overnight ❖ Correct seasonings to taste.

❖ *Serves 16.*

Note: To juice onion, purée roughly chopped onion in blender or food processor; twist into several layers of cheesecloth and squeeze, or just squeeze in a fist.

"Pleasing the Man" was the coy headline for a 1936 story on a classic mayonnaise-based sauce to serve with a mixed grill, once a common businessman's lunch, combining sizzling steak, kidneys, and a lamb or pork chop — and probably a martini or two. This cold sauce could also be served with grilled fish or vegetables.

Ravigote Sauce | Appeared Jan. 10, 1936

1   cup Homemade Mayonnaise (see page 10)
2   tablespoons cooked spinach, drained
      and chopped (about 1 cup fresh)
1   tablespoon capers, rinsed, drained,
      and chopped
3   anchovies, drained of oil
⅓   cup minced parsley
¼   cup minced fresh watercress leaves
Salt and freshly ground pepper

"Remember what you eat and drink today walks and talks and thinks tomorrow."

— *Prudence Penny, Nov. 2, 1932*

Combine all ingredients in a small bowl ❖ Cover, chill, and allow to season a few hours or overnight ❖ Correct seasonings to taste.

❖ *Makes about 1½ cups.*

Alumni of the all-male Saint Louis School who graduated in the 1950s and '60s fondly recall a "cafeteria lady" named Mrs. Tyau and the recipe they called "Mrs. Tyau's Dressing." When an *Advertiser* reader requested the recipe in 2006, Mrs. Tyau's sister called to say that the then 91-year-old Mrs. Tyau remembered making the stuff by the gallon. The boys liked it so much they put it on everything, not just salad. This rather sweet and unctuous mixture is a classic French dressing of the mid-twentieth century.

Mrs. Tyau's Dressing | Appeared April 19, 2006

1 (14.5-ounce) can tomato soup
1 cup salad oil
$\frac{1}{2}$ cup vinegar
$\frac{1}{4}$ cup sugar
1 teaspoon salt
1 teaspoon dry mustard
1 teaspoon paprika
3 tablespoons Worcestershire sauce
2 tablespoons grated onion
1 clove garlic, crushed and minced

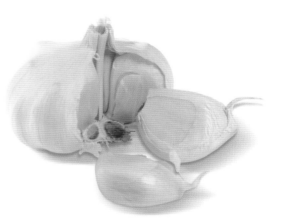

Combine all ingredients except garlic in blender and blend ❖ Add garlic and blend well.

❖ *Makes about 3 cups.*

This stir-fry sauce can be used in conventional stove-top recipes or with microwave "stir-fries," in which you microwave each ingredient in turn at the appropriate power and for an appropriate length of time, then add sauce and microwave just to heat through. The sauce makes enough for four meals for four people and keeps in the refrigerator in an airtight container for up to three weeks. Use about a cup for each recipe and vary the ingredients: meats, shrimp or tofu and whatever vegetables you like.

Stir-Fry Sauce | Appeared March 12, 2008

$2\frac{1}{2}$ cups chicken broth
$\frac{1}{2}$ cup soy sauce
$\frac{1}{2}$ cup light corn syrup
$\frac{1}{2}$ cup dry sherry
$\frac{1}{4}$ cup cider vinegar

2 garlic cloves, minced
2 teaspoons grated peeled fresh ginger
$\frac{1}{4}$ teaspoon cayenne (ground red pepper)
$\frac{1}{2}$ cup cornstarch whisked together with 6 tablespoons water to make a slurry

In a $1\frac{1}{2}$-quart jar with a tight-fitting lid or other suitable container, combine all ingredients except cornstarch ❖ Shake well ❖ Whisk in cornstarch slurry ❖ Shake again ❖ Refrigerate.

❖ *Makes 4 cups to serve 16.*

Variation:
- Instead of chicken broth, use dashi, mushroom broth, or beef broth.
- Instead of regular soy sauce, use low-sodium soy sauce or Bragg Liquid Aminos.
- Instead of corn syrup, substitute honey, molasses, brown rice syrup, or agave (cactus) syrup.
- In place of sherry, use sweet vermouth, sake, Shaohsing (Chinese rice wine), or Sauternes.
- Instead of cider vinegar, use Filipino-style vinegar made from cane sap, palm sugar, or coconut.
- Use more or less garlic or ginger.
- Instead of cayenne, use chili sauce, sambal oelek (Indonesian chile paste) or a mashed Hawaiian chile pepper.
- Use arrowroot in place of cornstarch.

Every kitchen needs a good teriyaki sauce recipe. This one is from chef Sal Salvado of Parker Ranch, once the largest cattle ranch in the United States, on the verdant hills of Waimea on the Big Island.

Parker Ranch Teriyaki Sauce | Appeared Oct. 26, 1977

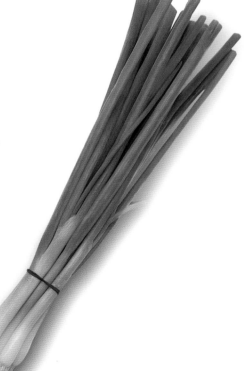

    ½   cup sugar
    ⅔   cup soy sauce
    3   tablespoons sherry
    2   tablespoons vegetable oil
    2   tablespoons toasted sesame seeds
    1   stalk green onions, chopped
    ½   teaspoon salt
    1   tablespoon grated ginger
    1   crushed garlic clove

Combine all ingredients in a covered jar and shake well ❖
Pour into covered container and marinate desired meats,
refrigerate, turning often ❖ Grill or broil meats ❖
While the meat is cooking, boil down the sauce
to drizzle over meats and rice!

❖ *Makes enough for 4 steaks or 4 servings
of thin-cut sukiyaki meat.*

Preserves and Pickles

Almost everyone loves the sweet but slightly resinous flavor of bananas. This easy banana jam can be served with breakfast breads, but also drizzled over pound cake or other plain cakes, stuffed into a dessert crêpe along with some cream cheese or crème fraîche, or paired with ice cream. Tiny, tart apple bananas would be great for this.

What's a hot water bath?

A canning kettle fitted with a rack is filled with water, which is brought to a boil. Filled and sealed sterile jars are lowered into water (use only canning jars and new lids; never recycled product jars). Timing begins once the water returns to a boil. You can make do with a soup pot; use tongs to lower jars into water. Canning supplies are at some grocery stores or online at Canning Pantry (www.canningpantry.com).

Tip

A single large mango, ¾ to 1 pound, yields about 1 cup sliced fruit. For a step-by-step guide to cutting a mango, go to Rachel Rappaport's excellent site, coconutlime.blogspot.com/2007/04/how-to-choose-and-prepare-mango.html.

Banana Jam | Appeared June 18, 1979

6   cups sliced, medium-ripe bananas
6   cups sugar (part brown sugar adds a layer of flavor)
1½ cups orange juice
¾   cup lemon juice

In a large, heavy saucepan, cook together bananas, sugar, and orange juice ❖ Bring to a boil, turn down heat to medium, and simmer 15 to 20 minutes, until thick ❖ To test for proper consistency, place a spoonful of the jam on a chilled saucer: it should sit up and not immediately release a lot of liquid ❖ Pour jam into sterilized jars and seal in hot water bath for 10 minutes or refrigerate.

❖ *Makes 4 to 6 (8-ounce) jars.*

Fresh mangoes are now in produce bins around the country, though we in the Islands think ours are best. To save work, look for large varieties with smooth-textured, not stringy flesh.

Mango Jam | Appeared May 22, 1985

4   cups water
12   cups ripe mango slices (about 12 large mangoes)
6   cups sugar

In a large pot over medium-high heat, combine water and mango slices ❖ Cook, simmering and stirring occasionally to prevent sticking, until mangoes are cooked through and softened, about 15 minutes ❖ Press mixture through sieve or purée in food processor ❖ Return to pot and add sugar ❖ Simmer over medium heat, stirring frequently, until mixture reaches jam consistency, about 30 minutes ❖ To test for proper consistency, place a spoonful of the jam on a chilled saucer: it should sit up and not immediately release a lot of its liquid ❖ Place in sterile canning jars and process in a hot water bath for 10 minutes.

❖ *Makes 6 (8-ounce) jars.*

Like most apple preserves, this chutney is best made with new-crop, tart cooking apples (e.g. Braeburn, Cortland, Criterion, Gravenstein, Granny Smith, Jonagold, pippin, Rome Beauty, Winesap), harvested in the fall (but with Australia in the market now, that means new-crop apples may be available to you in our spring, too).

Apple Chutney | Appeared Oct. 23, 2006

- 1 quart cider vinegar
- 10 cups cored, peeled, sliced cooking apples
- 4 cups brown sugar
- 1 cup chopped onion
- 1½ cups raisins
- 1 cup sliced dried figs, persimmons, or prunes

- 1 tablespoon salt
- 2 teaspoons ground ginger
- 2 tablespoons mixed pickling spice, tied in a cheesecloth bag
- 1 teaspoon cayenne pepper (optional; less if you don't care for spice)

Pour vinegar in a large, nonreactive kettle ❖ Slice peeled apples into vinegar so they won't discolor ❖ Combine remaining ingredients in pot with apples and stir to combine ❖ Bring slowly to a boil over medium heat, stirring frequently ❖ Reduce heat and simmer slowly, uncovered, for 2 hours, stirring occasionally ❖ Pack chutney in sterilized jars with lids ❖ Process in boiling water bath for 10 minutes ❖ Unsealed jars may be stored in refrigerator and will last for months.

❖ *Makes 8 (8-ounce) jars.*

Tip

Three medium apples weigh about 1 pound and produce about 3 cups of cored and sliced fruit.

Puckery, *pica* ("hot") pickled onions sat on the counter in recycled mayonnaise jars in most old-time Portuguese households. The pickles add character to salads and sandwiches, cut the richness of roast meats, and are a great *pau hana* (after-work) snack with beer. The pickles go together quickly, can be made in small batches (perhaps when onions are on sale), and may contain other vegetables (we've added carrots and peppers for color). This version, from a popular column of the '70s and '80s called "The Island Way," uses a characteristic pidgin English contraction — "pickle," instead of pickled.

Richard Kamakea's Portuguese Pickle Onion | Appeared Jan. 20, 1982

4-6 small white or sweet Maui onions
2   large carrots, cut in $\frac{1}{4}$-inch-thick rounds
1   bell pepper or parts of varied colors
2   garlic cloves, peeled and crushed
1   tablespoon Hawaiian salt
2   small, red hot Hawaiian chile peppers *(nīoi)*
1   tablespoon sugar (or a little more, to taste)
3   cups apple cider vinegar

Tip

To safely store pickled onions at room temperature, they must first be canned: use sterilized canning jars (not recycled jars) and fresh lids; process in boiling water bath 10 minutes.

Clean the onions of the papery skin ❖ Make shallow cuts to cut off the tops and bottoms ❖ Cut onions into neat eighths ❖ Fill a 1-quart canning jar with the onions, carrots, and bell pepper and set aside ❖ Make the pickling mixture: Seed and chop 1 chile pepper; leave the other whole ❖ Combine Hawaiian salt, chopped and whole chile peppers, sugar, and apple cider vinegar ❖ Fill jar two-thirds full of this mixture ❖ (Leftover mixture will keep for future use.) ❖ Fill remaining one-third of jar with water, leaving an inch of space ❖ Place a 4-inch square of waxed paper over jar top to prevent vinegar from corroding lid ❖ Cover tightly, shake well, and let stand 2 to 3 days to ripen ❖ Shake jar once daily ❖ Refrigerate after desired flavor is achieved.

❖ *Makes 1 quart, to serve about 12.*

Portuguese "Pickle" Onion is an old-time recipe that adds invigorating heat, piquancy and crunch to roast meats, in sandwiches or just by itself as a snack with beer.

"Sugar lands and other cultivated areas would be converted into food crops immediately upon indication of maritime dangers. Informed circles said that Hawaii would have emergency stores of rice, wheat, cattle feed, canned milk, and butter to supplement regular commercial supplies."

— July 2, 1941

If you enjoy making fruitcakes and have access to fresh, thick-skinned citrus (citron, oranges, or pomelos), you may wish to try making candied peel. Use only backyard or organically grown fruit to assure you aren't candying pesticides or other chemicals along with the peel. The best for this is citron (*Citrus medica*), found in some old Hawai'i gardens. Citron resembles a lemon on steroids — half a foot long — and are even more tart than lemons. It is primarily grown for its thick, bumpy rind, which has a lovely taste and texture when candied.

Candied Fruit Peel | Appeared Dec. 16, 1932

Whole citrus fruit (thick-skinned oranges, citron, or pomelo)
Water
Sugar

Wash and dry fruit ✣ Cut into halves and remove flesh; scrape away white inner rind ✣ Weigh fruit and record weight ✣ Cover peel with water and soak for 5 days in a cool place (air-conditioned room or refrigerator), changing water twice a day ✣ Drain, place in a large pot, cover with fresh cold water, and bring to a boil ✣ Reduce heat and simmer ✣ Drain and chop peel into small, even pieces ✣ In a pot, add equal parts of the peel's original dry weight in sugar and water ✣ (For example, if you had 1 pound of peel, you need 1 pound sugar and 2 cups water — 1 pound of water is 2 cups) ✣ Bring water and sugar to a boil; add peel and simmer gently for 1 hour; place in a cool place overnight ✣ Remove peel, return syrup to a boil, return peel to syrup, and repeat the cooking and marinating process ✣ Drain ✣ Dry peel before storing it: Preheat oven to 230 degrees ✣ Spread peel on a rimmed baking sheet and bake until peel has a candied texture throughout and appears translucent ✣ Store in an airtight plastic or glass container to prevent hardening.

For many, it's not a truly Korean meal unless it includes the pungent fermented vegetable known as kim chee, often made with cabbage but also with many other ingredients. Cucumber kim chee is an easy-to-make fresh version often offered as a complimentary relish in Korean and other local restaurants. This is my interpretation of Honoluluan Julia Chung's recipe; she was 89 when I talked to her in 2005 and said she didn't measure anymore: "After you make it so many times, you learn."

❋ Cucumber Kim Chee | Appeared July 20, 2005

2   Japanese cucumbers
Table salt or finely ground sea salt
1   teaspoon coarse-ground *kochukaru* (Korean red pepper)
1   tablespoon sugar
1   teaspoon minced garlic
1   teaspoon peeled, minced ginger
2   tablespoons (or more, as desired) minced green onion

Wash unpeeled cucumber, cut off ends and cut into chunks ✣ In a nonreactive bowl, layer the chunks with a light sprinkling of salt between each layer ✣ Toss and stir to distribute salt ✣ Allow to sit for 20 minutes, then rinse off a piece and taste ✣ If too salty, wash cucumber in cold water and proceed ✣ If not salty enough, allow to marinate longer ✣ When the flavor is right, drain and rinse in cold water ✣ In a bowl, stir together *kochukaru*, sugar, garlic, ginger, and green onion ✣ Add cucumber, toss well, and pack into sterilized jars ✣ Refrigerate; this is ready to eat the same day ✣ Keeps about 2 weeks, refrigerated.

✣ *Serves 6 to 8.*

Breads and Crackers

Batter breads are quick yeast breads — as little as a couple of hours from cupboard to counter. They allow you to enjoy the smell and wholesome flavor of yeast breads without the time and mess of kneading (the soft batter is beaten with a wooden spoon or mixer rather than worked by hand). This recipe offers the taste of buttery, fruit-rich panettone, the Milanese Christmas loaf, but with more fiber and less sugar and fat. It is a dense flattish loaf somewhere between a breakfast bar and a coffee cake. Use no more than ¾ cup total dried fruit or the bread will be too heavy, and don't omit the salt. Use any dried fruit, so long as it's finely chopped; butter is optional; reduce the sugar by half or use Splenda for the batter (but real sugar is required in the sponge to "feed" the yeast; moisten the batter with almost any liquid.

Baked Oatmeal alla Panettone | Appeared April 30, 2008

For the sauce:
- $1/2$ cup all-purpose flour or whole wheat pastry flour or half of each
- 2 tablespoons brown sugar
- 2 tablespoons active dry yeast
- $3/4$ cup very warm water, milk, or other liquid

For the bread:
- $1/2$ cup all-purpose flour or whole wheat pastry flour or half of each
- 2 tablespoons brown sugar or Splenda Brown Sugar Blend
- $1/4$ teaspoon salt
- Finely grated zest of 1 orange
- 2 eggs or $1/2$ cup egg substitute, beaten
- 2 tablespoons melted butter, margarine, or vegetable oil (optional)
- 1 teaspoon lemon extract
- 1 teaspoon almond extract
- 1 teaspoon vanilla extract
- $1/4$ cup candied fruit (citron or orange peel preferred)
- $1/4$ cup raisins, currants, or sultanas (dried white seedless grapes)
- $1/4$ cup dried sweetened cranberries (Craisins, if available)
- 1.5 ounces slivered almonds (5 tablespoons)
- 2 cups old-fashioned rolled oatmeal

Make a sponge: In a large bowl, whisk together ½ cup flour, 2 tablespoons brown sugar, yeast, and warm liquid ❖ Cover with a light towel and allow to "proof" (rise) in a warm place for 30 minutes, until the mixture is puffy ❖ Coat an 8 x 8–inch baking pan, a 9-inch round or 5 (3 x 5–inch) mini loaf pans with vegetable oil spray ❖ Set aside.

Make the bread: Preheat oven to 350 degrees ❖ In a medium bowl, combine additional flour, sugar or Splenda, salt, zest, eggs, melted butter, and extracts; add the sponge and beat vigorously several minutes with mixer or wooden spoon ❖ Stir fruit, nuts, and oatmeal into mixture and mix well ❖ Place the batter in prepared pan or pans, sprinkle a few more slivered almonds over the top, lightly cover with a towel and place on top of stove (not on the burner that vents heat from the oven) ❖ Allow to proof (froth and puff up a bit) for 30 to 40 minutes, just until the batter puffs and rises a little ❖ Bake for 20 to 35 minutes (depending on size of pan), until toothpick emerges clean from the center ❖ Do not overbake ❖ Cool on rack ❖ Keeps 1 week in a zippered plastic bag in the refrigerator.

❖ *Serves 12.*

When David Eyre died at 95 in 2008, the first line of his obituary was predictable: "David W. Eyre traveled the world, edited magazines, wrote books, and served as a spokesman for one of Hawai'i's largest companies. But it was a pancake recipe that made him famous." That's because Eyre once entertained New York Times food editor Craig Claiborne and served this version of the old-time Dutch baby as an unusual (and ridiculously easy) dessert. Claiborne printed the recipe and it became the most requested of any he ever published. Serve it for breakfast with powdered sugar and fruit, or for dessert with fruit sloshed with Grand Marnier, Cointreau, or Chambord.

David Eyre's Pancake | Appeared June 28, 2000

½ cup flour
½ cup milk
2 eggs
½ teaspoon nutmeg
4 tablespoons butter
3-4 tablespoons powdered sugar
Juice of ½ lemon (about 1 tablespoon)

Preheat oven to 425 degrees ✤ In a mixing bowl, combine the flour, milk, eggs, and nutmeg ✤ Beat until well mixed, but don't mind the lumps ✤ Melt the butter in an 11-inch aluminum skillet with a heatproof handle, or a 7 x 11–inch baking dish ✤ Pour batter into the skillet and place in oven for 20 minutes, or until pancake puffs and turns golden brown ✤ Sprinkle top with sugar and lemon juice ✤ Return pancake to oven for a few minutes, just enough to allow the topping to amalgamate ✤ Garnish with fruit and whipped cream, if desired.

✤ *Serves 2 to 4.*

David Eyre's Pancake, the Dutch Baby that put an Island gourmet on the national map via Craig Claiborne's New York Times column, makes a dramatic but easy dessert.

A reader requested this light-textured, crisp lahvosh, once served at the Banker's Club at First Hawaiian Bank. We can see why: it's rich with milk, eggs, and butter. Note that the dough is prepared 2 days in advance of baking.

Lahvosh | Appeared Aug. 5, 1998

8   cups flour (or mixed whole wheat and all-purpose flours)
1   tablespoon sugar
1   teaspoon salt
1   pound butter or margarine, at room temperature
3   eggs
3   cups whole or skim milk
White sesame seeds and poppy seeds

In a large mixing bowl, combine flour, sugar, and salt, and mix together ❖ Cut butter into dry ingredients until mixture resembles coarse meal ❖ In a medium bowl, beat together eggs and milk ❖ Make a well in the center of the flour and butter mixture ❖ Pour milk-and-egg mixture into well and mix thoroughly ❖ Cover bowl with clear plastic wrap and refrigerate for 2 days (this makes it easier to roll out) ❖ On serving day, preheat oven to 300 degrees ❖ Spray a cookie sheet with cooking oil ❖ Roll dough out very thin, fitting it to the size of the cookie sheet ❖ Spray dough with water, wetting it completely; poke holes in the dough with the tines of a fork ❖ Sprinkle with seeds ❖ With a pizza cutter or sharp knife, cut dough into squares of desired size ❖ Bake on an ungreased cookie sheet for 15 minutes, until golden brown.

❖ *Serves 8 to 10.*

The Plantation Village in Waipahu fired up its wood-burning forno (Portuguese-style masonry oven) in 2006 for chef Alan Wong, who was planning a fundraiser celebrating Hawai'i's ethnic foods. The original idea was to make buttery rich sweet bread, but I persuaded Wong and pastry chef Mark Okumura to try instead the everyday breads of the Portuguese — crusty white milk bread and broa, a savory corn bread that pairs well with soup. Here's my broa recipe, baked in a 9-inch cake or pie pan.

Broa: Portuguese Corn Bread | From Wanda's Kitchen

- 1 package active dry yeast
- 1 teaspoon sugar
- 1¼ cups warm water (110-115 degrees), divided
- ¾ cup warm milk
- 1 teaspoon salt
- 2 cups yellow cornmeal, processed in a food processor or blender until very fine
- 3 cups flour (or half all-purpose and half whole wheat pastry flour)

Preheat oven to 350 degrees ❖ In a small bowl, combine yeast, sugar, and ¼ cup warm water and allow to "proof" (froth and puff up a bit) ❖ Meanwhile, in a large bowl, mix remaining water, milk, and salt ❖ Add yeast mixture when proofed, then beat in flour and cornmeal, ½-cup at a time until you have a soft but not sticky dough ❖ Sprinkle counter or board with flour, turn out dough, and knead until smooth; 5 minutes or so ❖ Butter a medium bowl, place dough in bowl, cover with plastic wrap or light kitchen towel and rise in a warm place for one hour ❖ Punch down and form into round; place in buttered 9-inch cake or pie pan and cover with light towel to rise again ❖ Bake for 40 minutes or slightly longer ❖ Loaf should sound hollow when it's thumped and internal temperature should be 190 degrees when checked with an instant-read thermometer.

❖ *Makes 1 round loaf to serve 6 to 8.*

Snacks

Though the backyard mango tree is rapidly becoming a nostalgic memory, determined Islanders can usually manage to cadge some free green mangoes off a relative or neighbor, or find the fruit in a farmers' market or in Chinatown on O'ahu. Use the mangoes to make chutney and bright red slivers of pickled mango — a delicacy of the sweet-sour sort that, if you've ever eaten it, causes your mouth to water just at the thought. Mangoes may be seeded and sliced while in season and frozen in zippered plastic bags for later use in this and other recipes.

Pickled Mango | Appeared July 4, 1990

    4   quarts green mango, sliced about
           1/2 inch wide (about 16 mangoes)
    3   cups water
    2 1/2 cups brown sugar
    1 3/4 cups vinegar
    1/4 cup Hawaiian or kosher salt
    1/2 teaspoon 5-spice powder
    1   tablespoon red food coloring

Place mango slices in 4 sterilized 1-quart canning jars ❖
In a saucepan, combine remaining ingredients; bring to a boil ❖
Carefully pour liquid over mangoes, cap with clean lids and allow to stand at room temperature for 24 hours ❖ Store in refrigerator ❖ Mangoes are then ready to munch and will keep for several months.

❖ *Makes 4 quarts.*

Islanders love sweet potatoes; delis sell chunks of plain boiled or baked sweet potatoes for snacking. But this is a much more decadent treatment: sweet potato chips. The key is to slice the potatoes very thinly. Try these with a dip made of blended chutney and softened cream cheese, sprinkle with seasoned salt, or use purple Okinawan or Moloka'i sweet potatoes.

Sweet Potato Chips | Appeared March 21, 1984

    3/4 pounds sweet potatoes, washed   Vegetable oil for frying   Salt

Peel sweet potatoes and very thinly slice crosswise (the food processor is useful for this) ❖ Immerse in ice water for 15 minutes; drain thoroughly and pat dry with paper towels ❖ In a deep fryer or a heavy-bottomed Dutch oven or frying pan, heat at least 3 inches vegetable oil to 350 degrees ❖ Fry potatoes in batches, not crowding them, until delicate brown; drain on paper towels; sprinkle with salt and serve immediately.

❖ *Serves 3 to 4.*

Except for folks from the Deep South, who also eat boiled peanuts, most non-Islanders find the very concept of a boiled peanut exceedingly strange. But the texture, similar to that of al dente pasta, and the elusive trace of licorice and powerful hit of salt makes them a favorite *pau hana* (after-work) snack. In the old days, you'd buy them in damp paper sacks and munch them at the movies, scattering the shells heedlessly on the floor.

❋ Boiled Peanuts | Appeared Sept. 5, 1983

1	pound raw unshelled peanuts	12	cups water
2	whole star anise	$1/2$	cup Hawaiian or kosher salt

Rinse peanuts well ❖ Place them in a large soup pot and add anise, water, and salt ❖ Bring to a boil and simmer gently for 2 to 3 hours ❖ After 2 hours, taste a nut to check texture and saltiness ❖ If too salty, add water; if not salty enough, add another ¼ cup salt ❖ Add water, if necessary, to keep peanuts submerged.

See mui, Chinese preserved fruit, was the candy of Island childhoods. We called it "crack seed," referring to the seed or kernel inside that had been cracked to add flavor, though plums and other fruit were often prepared with the whole seed at the center. We'd make the "seed" last by first daintily nibbling the rippled salty-sweet edges, sucking on the seed, rolling it around in our mouths. Many seeds are made with *li hing* powder (a spice mixture of dried plums, sugar, salt, licorice, flavorings, and aspartame). Before *li hing* powder became widely available, home cooks made their "seed" snacks by borrowing the flavor from commercial products. This recipe makes a ton of treats, suitable for holiday giving. Store in an airtight container.

❋ Fruit Mui | Appeared June 20, 1984

8	(12-ounce) packages pitted prunes	1	pound brown sugar
3	tablespoons Hawaiian salt	3	tablespoons whiskey
$1/2$	pound lemon peel (sweet-sour lemon)	2	whole star anise
$1/2$	pound *li hing mui* (dried plum)	$1 1/4$	cups lemon juice
1	tablespoon 5-spice powder		

In a large plastic container with an airtight lid, combine all ingredients and mix well ❖ Soak for a minimum of 2 days, stirring occasionally ❖ Pack in clean jars or plastic containers.

Variations: Replace all or part of the prunes with dried apricots, peaches, apples, or dried persimmons in bite-size pieces, quartered dried figs, or other mixed dried fruit.

Tip

Lemon peel and *li hing* powder are available online at Crack Seed Center (www.crackseedcenter.com).

With roots mostly in Asia, salty and sweet snacks are a distinctly Island-style tradition. Some of these — *arare* rice crackers and rolled cuttlefish, for example — aren't made at home, but many others are. And innovative local cooks have created dozens of second- and third-generation variations on the original themes. This crunchy treat, a relative of a Japanese confection made with sugar but no butter, characterizes this trend.

Okoshi: Puffed Rice Candy | Appeared Aug. 23, 1990

8	cups puffed rice cereal (not Rice Krispies)
1	cup unsalted roasted peanuts
½	cup butter or margarine
1	cup sugar
¼	cup corn syrup

Lightly butter a 9 x 13–inch pan; set aside. Preheat oven to 250 degrees ❖ Spread cereal and peanuts in a rimmed baking pan (or 2, if needed) ❖ Toast cereal and peanuts a few minutes until crisp ❖ Pour into a large bowl ❖ In a saucepan over medium heat, combine butter or margarine, sugar, and corn syrup and cook, stirring constantly, until golden brown and thickened (15 to 20 minutes) ❖ Pour butter mixture over cereal and peanuts and mix ❖ Scrape into prepared 9 x 13–inch pan and press with buttered hands, or cover with waxed paper and press until even ❖ Cool slightly but not all the way; cut into squares. (If you let it cool all the way, it becomes difficult to cut.)

❖ *Serves 10 to 12.*

Home Away from Homeland

A reader wrote to request a recipe for Portuguese sausage for her son, who lives away from the Islands and can't get our favorite garlicky linguiça near his home. I sent a simple recipe, but have worked on it since, pumping up the spices. This recipe is just right for a small household, and relatively easy to make, particularly if you make patties rather than filling sausage casings. The degree of garlic and spice is up to your taste; the sausages can range from very mild to quite lively.

Portuguese Sausage | Appeared Nov. 15, 2006

    1   pound Boston pork butt, the fattier the better
    3-6 cloves garlic, peeled and minced
    Dash cayenne (crushed red pepper), to taste
    1   teaspoon Hawaiian or kosher salt
    2   tablespoons white or cider vinegar or lemon juice
    2   teaspoons Portuguese 5-Spice Powder (recipe follows)
    1   tablespoon paprika

Chop pork into ¼-inch cubes, place in large bowl, and stir to distribute fat through the meat ❖ In a blender or mini food processor, purée together the garlic, red pepper, salt, vinegar or lemon juice, and Portuguese 5-Spice ❖ Add to pork and stir well. Cover airtight, refrigerate 12 hours, stirring 3 or 4 times ❖ Pinch off a bit of the sausage mixture, fry, and taste. Correct seasonings to taste ❖ Form into patties or fill clean casings according to sausage-making directions.

❖ *Makes about a dozen patties or 10 small sausage links.*

Variation: Substitute 1-3 small, hot red peppers (Hawaiian *nīoi* or Thai bird chiles) for the cayenne, or use ¼-2 teaspoons red chile paste (such as sambal oelek).

Portuguese 5-Spice Powder

    1   tablespoon cinnamon
    1   tablespoon cloves
    1   tablespoon black pepper

    1   bay leaf, crumbled (see Note)
    1   whole star anise or 1 tablespoon
        ground anise (see Note)

Grind ingredients in a blender or spice grinder or crush to a powder with a Thai-style stone mortar and pestle ❖ Before using, measure out the amount you need and toast in a dry frying pan over medium-high heat, swirling or stirring often, until fragrance is released.

❖ *Makes about ¼ cup.*

Note: Some recipes call for fennel instead of bay and aniseeds in place of star anise.

Gau, a chewy, gooey Chinese sweet rice pudding, is to Chinese New Year as fruitcake is to Christmas. It's purchased at Chinese bakeries or made at home. Slivers of the sticky, pudding-like cake are served with tea. When teaching cooking to Narcissus Queen candidates, Linda Chang Wyrgatsch, a Pearl City homemaker and artist, adapted the fruity gau of her native Shanghai to speedy preparation in the microwave.

Linda's Speedy Shanghai Gau | Appeared Feb. 2, 2005

    12 ounces dried red dates (about 1 cup)
    1   pound mochiko (sweet rice flour)
    3/4 cup sugar
    1/2 cup salad oil
    3/4-1 cup water
    1/2 cup pine nuts

In a saucepan, cover dates with water ❖ Bring to a boil, lower heat and cook for 45 minutes, or until dates are soft; drain ❖ Remove pits ❖ Line a 10 x 5–inch microwave-safe baking dish with plastic wrap ❖ In a bowl, combine mochiko, sugar, oil, and water; mix well ❖ Stir in dates and nuts ❖ Pour mixture into prepared dish; cover with plastic wrap ❖ Microwave on High for 7 minutes, rotating dish several times during cooking ❖ With a flexible spatula or your fingers, carefully turn *gau* over ❖ Microwave on High another 3 minutes ❖ Let stand, uncovered, for about 30 minutes ❖ Pull *gau* from sides of dish and invert onto platter ❖ Cool and cut into serving pieces.

❖ *Serves 20.*

CHAPTER 2

Pūpū and Potluck

DISHES FOR
ISLAND-STYLE PARTIES

ong before "small plate" and "tapas" restaurants became fashionable, Islanders were making meals of the appetizers we call *pūpū* — a word that refers both to small shells and to the tidbits served along with the mildly intoxicating drink made from the kava root. But *pūpū* today are far from tidbits; instead, most local parties consist of "heavy *pūpū*" meaning there's so many and so much that you won't need dinner later. And if the dish you take to a potluck serves less than 12 — *pohō* (waste time)!

Pūpū

In the 1950s, Coral brand tuna was canned in Hawai'i and the industry celebrated with an annual Tuna Week. Tuna Week in 1952 gave birth to this recipe.

Tuna Lemon Pâte | Appeared Oct. 2, 1952

1	(7-ounce) can tuna in oil, drained
6	slices bacon, fried crisp and crumbled
6	tablespoons mayonnaise
2	teaspoons lemon juice
1/2	teaspoon lemon zest
	Red Pepper Sauce (Tabasco Sauce, if available), to taste
1/4	teaspoon salt
	Pepper to taste

> "Use tuna when there's nothing for the family."
> — *July 21, 1933*

In a bowl, blend pâte ingredients ❖ Correct seasonings to taste ❖ Chill ❖ Serve with crostini or crackers ❖ Makes 1½ cups.

❖ *Makes 8 to 10 as an appetizer.*

At brunch at Daniel Thiebaut restaurant in Waimea a while back, my brother gave me a new nickname: "Gin-jah." This was because he guessed the last key ingredient in the outrageously good *poke* we were enjoying. *Poke* (PO-kay) is a raw tuna mélange and a Native Hawaiian favorite. Here's the version I came up with after we got home. Even Mainlanders should be able to find all the ingredients for this.

 Garlic Poke | Appeared July 4, 2007

> 1 pound raw 'ahi tuna, in bite-size squares
> ½ tablespoon sesame oil
> 1½ tablespoons soy sauce, or to taste
> 2 teaspoons Hawaiian or kosher salt (see Note)
> 2 teaspoons grated fresh ginger
> 3 tablespoons chopped macadamia nuts
> 2-3 tablespoons minced green onion
> 2-3 tablespoons minced red onion
> 1½ tablespoons minced garlic
> *Furikake* (Japanese seaweed seasoning mixture; optional)

Combine all ingredients except *furikake* in a large bowl ✜ Cover and marinate, refrigerated, for 1 hour or longer ✜ Sprinkle with *furikake* just before serving.

✜ *Serves 6 as an appetizer.*

Note: Recipe may be doubled or tripled except for salt; taste and add as desired to expanded recipe.

What's *furikake*?

Furikake (foo-rih-KAH-kay) is a Japanese seasoning of crisp dried seaweed, sesame seeds, salt, and other ingredients; there are many versions. As a garnish in many dishes, it adds crunch and a briny saltiness. Many Islanders make a snack of a bowl of hot rice topped with *furikake*.

In 1985, the *Advertiser*, under the able direction of food editor Mary Cooke, released *Taste of Hawaii*, a cookbook that compiled reader contributions made to Maili Yardley's "The Island Way" column and the long-running monthly "Coping with Cost" feature. On the day the cookbook was released, this creamy and slightly sweet recipe appeared in the newspaper to tease potential buyers' appetites.

Mango Dip | Appeared Oct. 23, 1985

1	cup sliced fresh mango, drained on paper towels (about 1 mango)
1	(3-ounce) package cream cheese (low-fat is okay)
1	cup sour cream (light is okay)
3/4	teaspoon lime juice
1/2	teaspoon grated orange rind

In a blender or food processor, process mango until smooth ❖ Place mango in bowl and beat in remaining ingredients ❖ Blend well and chill ❖ Serve with apples, pears or Asian pears, jícama (chop suey yam), or thin crackers.

❖ *Makes 12 to 16 as an appetizer.*

There was never a time in my childhood when canned corned beef wasn't stacked high in my grandmother's cupboard. Corned beef was a hedge against disasters, great and small: everything from being stranded in case the bridge washed out in the valley where we lived (that happened once) to a busy day when Grandma had little time to make dinner. Besides, we loved the stuff. Here's a *pūpū* guaranteed to please the *pau hana* (after-work) beer-and-chips crowd.

Kama'āina Corned Beef Spread | From Wanda's Kitchen

1	(12-ounce) can corned beef	1/2	cup minced green onion
1/2	cup mayonnaise	1	teaspoon garlic powder
1/2	cup sour cream	1/8	teaspoon chile pepper water or
1	(3-ounce) envelope ranch dressing mix		few drops liquid hot pepper seasoning
3	ounces cream cheese, softened		(e.g. Tabasco Sauce)

In a bowl, mash corned beef well with a potato masher or two strong forks; smooth, breaking up all lumps ❖ Stir in remaining ingredients, mixing well ❖ Correct seasonings to taste ❖ Serve with sliced French bread, crisp garlic toasts, or old-fashioned saloon pilot crackers or soda crackers.

❖ *Serves 8 or more as an appetizer.*

Is it an appetizer dip or a dessert spread? Yes. You can use this versatile mango mixture either way — spread on crisp fruit or jicama, or sandwiched between a pair of plain cookies, or even old-fashioned cream crackers!

Nori Chicken — morsels of boneless chicken thigh ringed with crisp rolled seaweed — is a beloved dish in Hilo, where it's sold in every okazu-ya (Japanese deli) and people debate which restaurant's version is best. For the home cook, it tends to be party food because it's a lot of work — only worth it when company's coming. This version was contributed by Janet Martin, born and raised in Hilo. Don't be intimidated: the nori-wrapping process is easier than it sounds, just a bit tedious. The chicken can be prepared an hour or so ahead of time and served at room temperature.

 ### Nori Chicken | Appeared Sept. 26, 1990

2½ pounds boneless chicken thighs
¾ cup cornstarch
¾ cup mochiko (sweet rice flour)
¾ cup sugar
½ teaspoon salt
2-4 cloves garlic, minced
⅓ cup finely minced green onion
2 eggs, lightly beaten

⅓ cup soy sauce
1 tablespoon kochujang (Korean hot bean paste)
1 (28-ounce) package nori (paper-thin black seaweed sheets)
Oil for deep-frying
Dipping Sauce (recipe follows)

Cut thighs crosswise into 40 strips about 1-1½ x 2-2½ inches, trimming away fat and gristle ❖ In a container with a cover, combine cornstarch, mochiko, sugar, and salt; mix well ❖ Stir in garlic, green onions, eggs, soy sauce, and kochujang ❖ Cover and marinate chicken overnight in refrigerator ❖ With scissors, cut nori sheets into 40 strips, 1 x 5 inches; to save time, cut multiple sheets at once ❖ In a heavy frying pan or Dutch oven, heat 2 inches of vegetable oil to 350 degrees (use a clip-on candy thermometer) ❖ Line 2 plates with paper towels, one to work over and one on which the fried chicken will drain ❖ Place some water in a small bowl ❖ Wrap a piece of chiken in a nori strip; dip a finger in the water, wipe across nori end, and press to adhere ❖ Repeat to prepare 5 or 6 pieces of wrapped chicken; fry them while you prepare the next five or six pieces ❖ Fry chicken until it is quite brown to ensure that the interior is cooked through ❖ Drain on paper towel-lined plate ❖ Serve nori-wrapped chicken hot or at room temperature with Dipping Sauce.

❖ *Serves 20 as an appetizer.*

Nori Chicken Dipping Sauce

¼ cup soy sauce
2 tablespoons water

Juice of 1 lemon
1 tablespoon minced green onion

⅛ teaspoon minced or grated fresh ginger

Just before serving, in a bowl, combine all ingredients.

❖ *Makes about ½ cup, to serve 15 to 20.*

Parties mean *pūpū*, like this Hilo favorite, Nori Chicken: marinated chicken breast wrapped in strips of crackling, briny seaweed and deep-fried.

A 1969 *Advertiser* special section featuring ethnic recipes included one for beef lumpia (LOOM-pee-ah), a favorite Philippine appetizer resembling Vietnamese spring rolls or Chinese egg rolls. As many of us are seeking healthy alternatives to fatty foods these days, lettuce can take the place of the traditional lumpia pasta wrap, and tofu or commercial soy "burger" (e.g. Boca brand) are lighter substitutes for beef. You can make your own Tofu Crumbles as well (recipe follows).

 ### Low-Fat Lettuce Leaf "Lumpia" | Appeared Oct. 23, 1969

For the tofu crumbles (see Note):
- 1 block firm tofu
- 1/3 cup whole wheat flour
- Salt and pepper
- 1 tablespoon oil for frying
- 2 tablespoons soy sauce
- 2 tablespoons cider vinegar

Lumpia Dipping Sauce (recipe follows)
Green or red leaf lettuce leaves, washed and spun or patted dry
Flat chives, blanched and shocked with ice water to stop the cooking

For filling:
- 1/2 cup minced onion
- 1/2 cup minced green onions
- 1/2 cup minced water chestnuts
- 1/2 cup bean sprouts
- 1/2 cup grated carrot or carrot matchsticks
- 1/2 cup green beans, tips trimmed and cut into 1/4-inch pieces
- 1 tablespoon soy sauce
- 1 tablespoon Philippine-style cane vinegar or cider vinegar
- 2 cloves garlic, minced
- 1 tablespoon patis (fish sauce)

Make the tofu crumbles: Place tofu on a plate and compress with a flat plate stacked with canned goods ❖ Compress for 30 minutes, allowing liquid to drain off; pour off liquid ❖ Cut into 1/3-inch dice ❖ Place flour in large flat pan or baking dish, sprinkle liberally with salt and pepper, and dredge tofu in flour ❖ In a nonstick frying pan, heat oil over medium heat ❖ Fry half the tofu pieces in a single layer, shaking and turning with a rubber spatula until pieces are golden on all sides ❖ Drizzle half the soy sauce and cider vinegar (or Philippine vinegar) over tofu and season well with pepper ❖ Repeat with remaining tofu.

In a large bowl, toss together tofu nuggets, onions, green onions, water chestnuts, bean sprouts, carrots, green beans, soy sauce, vinegar, garlic, and fish sauce ❖ Marinate 1/2 hour at room temperature.

Coat a medium to large frying pan with cooking oil spray, heat over medium-high heat, and quickly stir-fry marinated lumpia filling just until heated through and a little bit caramelized; vegetables should still be crisp ❖ Place individual lettuce leaves on a flat surface; place 2 to 3 tablespoons of filling on each lettuce leaf and roll; tie with blanched chives ❖ Arrange on platter with bowl of dipping sauce.

❖ *Makes about 24 rolls, to serve 12.*

Note: Alternatively, use 1 pound of store-bought tofu crumbles. Recipe for homemade tofu crumbles based on an idea from Dr. Terri Shintani.

Lettuce bundles, bound with ribbons of chive, encase a filling that tastes like that of the favorite Filipino party food, lumpia, but contains a lot less fat than the conventional recipe, which is made with deep-fried wrappers.

Lumpia Dipping Sauce

½ cup shoyu
¼ cup calamansi (Philippine lime) or lemon juice
Patis (fish sauce)

Variation:

For conventional lumpia, stir-fry 1 pound ground beef; drain fat. In the same frying pan, stir-fry remaining filling ingredients as above. Cool. Place a tablespoon or so of filling on a lumpia wrapper (square spring roll shell). Fold in opposite sides, roll jelly-roll-style and seal with a little dab of water. Deep-fry at 375 degrees for 3 minutes. Drain on paper towels and serve warm.

Fish sauce

Fish sauce is used throughout Southeast Asia as both an ingredient and a dipping sauce. In each region, the sauce, made from fermented fish or shellfish, has a different name and a slightly different flavor and intensity, though they may be used interchangeably. Don't be intimidated by the flavor and aroma of the fish sauce alone; like anchovies in European cooking, fish sauce offers an interesting background character when combined with other ingredients. Some names to look for: patis (Philippines), nam pla (Thailand), nuoc mam (Vietnam).

This rich, textured seafood spread was a signature at Hoku's at the ritzy Kahala Hotel & Resort when the fine dining restaurant opened in 1994, served with house-made flatbreads from their wood-burning or tandoori ovens. It was the creation of then executive chef Oliver Altherr, a *Food & Wine* magazine 1998 Best New Chef now working in Europe. 'Ahi Poke Dip fuses the ingredients of *poke* with pickled ginger and sesame seeds from the East, mayonnaise and white pepper from the West. Recipe may be halved if yours is not a large party.

 ## 'Ahi Poke Dip | Appeared June 11, 1997

1½ cups mayonnaise
½ cup béni shoga (shredded pink pickled ginger), drained
  (store-bought or homemade; see How to make pickled ginger)
½ cup minced green onion
½ cup minced cilantro
¼ cup toasted sesame seeds
½ cup lemon juice
½ cup soy sauce
¾ cup finely minced 'ahi (fresh raw yellowfin tuna; medium grade is fine)
2 teaspoons white pepper

In a bowl, combine all ingredients except 'ahi ✤ Refrigerate, tightly covered. Just before serving, add 'ahi and season with pepper ✤ Correct seasonings to taste.

✤ *Makes 4 to 5 cups.*

A "cocktail" of creamy 'ahi tuna dip with a crisp baguette slice is a restaurant idea that translates ready to the home table for special occasions. Try the same recipe with cold-smoked salmon.

Béni shoga

Béni shoga, or gari, is shredded ginger, tinted pink and pickled. You can purchase it bottled or in plastic containers, or make your own (recipe follows).

How to make pickled ginger

Peel and julienne a couple of hand-length segments of young fresh ginger. Soak in water to cover with 1 teaspoon salt for 1 hour. Rinse in colander in cold, running water; drain well, pressing water out. In a saucepan, make pickling mixture of 1 cup rice vinegar, 3 tablespoons sugar, and 1 teaspoon salt; heat until sugar dissolves. Add a drop of red food coloring and immerse ginger in hot pickling mixture. Place in airtight container, refrigerate for 24 hours before use (keeps almost indefinitely).

Tip

Another, very different but at least equally delicious tuna-based spread, created by current executive chef Wayne Hirabayashi, is served at Hoku's tables now — worth a visit.

Alyssa Moreau, a Honolulu private chef who specializes in healthful vegetarian meals and teaches classes in flavorful vegetarian cooking, gave me this recipe some years ago. The rest of the country has now discovered edamame (fresh soy beans), a pleasing source of protein.

Hummus Edamame | From Wanda's Kitchen

1½ cups shelled, cooked edamame
1   tablespoon olive oil
½   teaspoon salt
½   teaspoon cumin
¼   teaspoon coriander
2   cloves garlic, minced (or to taste)
½   cup minced Italian (flat-leaf) parsley
3   tablespoons tahini
         (ground sesame seed paste)
3   tablespoons water
3   tablespoons fresh lemon juice
1   teaspoon fruity extra-virgin olive oil
½   teaspoon paprika

In a food processor fitted with the steel blade, purée all ingredients but olive oil and paprika until smooth ❖ Spoon into serving bowl and drizzle with olive oil and sprinkle with paprika ❖ Serve with lahvosh, crackers, or thin-sliced jícama (known in Hawai'i as the Chinese potato).

❖ *Serves 12 as an appetizer.*

Potluck Dishes

Chili is a dish about which everyone has particular opinions. I like pretty much any kind of chili, with and without beans, vegetarian or with meat, spicy or bland. As an Islander, however, I insist it be served over rice, preferably with a dusting of sharp Cheddar. This spicy, meaty creation is my answer to the fanatics who think beans in chili are abomination. It's an all-day project but takes care after itself after the ingredients are combined, simmering on the stove. It serves a crowd.

Chipotle en adobo

Chipotle en adobo is a canned mixture of grilled chipotle peppers and an extremely spicy tomato sauce. It adds a smoky heat to all manner of recipes.

Wanda's Chili | From Wanda's Kitchen

1-2 tablespoon olive oil
3½ pounds beef chuck blade roast or
     similar cut, in bite-size chunks
Ground black pepper
½ medium onion, chopped (about ¾ cup)
4 cloves garlic, minced
1 teaspoon oregano
1 teaspoon cumin
1 teaspoon ground black pepper
1 jalapeño pepper, seeded and minced

1 Anaheim chile, seeded and minced
   (about 2 ounces)
1 pasilla chile (about 4 ounces), seeded,
   halved, broiled skin-side up until
   blistered, peeled, and roughly chopped
4 cups water
1 (7-ounce) can chipotle en adobo, puréed
   (or half a can for less spice)
6 slices bacon, cut into strips
1 teaspoon salt (or to taste)

Heat olive oil until shimmering ❖ Add beef in batches, liberally dusted with pepper, and brown 3 to 4 minutes ❖ Remove beef and set aside ❖ Over medium heat in same pot, add onion, garlic, oregano, cumin, and chiles and fry until onion is limp and translucent ❖ Return meat to pot and add the water ❖ Bring to a boil, reduce heat to medium and simmer 3 hours ❖ Add ¼ cup puréed *chipotle en adobo*, bacon, and salt ❖ Simmer 1 hour; correct adobo and other seasonings to taste ❖ Simmer for another 1 to 2 hours.

❖ *Serves 8 to 10.*

In 1989, the wife of newly elected Honolulu mayor Frank Fasi, Joyce Kono Fasi, a University of Hawai'i home economics graduate (1958) talked to the *Advertiser* about managing a blended family that included a total of 12 around the table each night (she and Fasi had 6 children together, and he had children from a previous marriage as well). She had to learn to cook Italian food and His Honor would actually "grade" her spaghetti sauce. Finally, she mastered the following recipe and got the Fasi "shaka" of approval. For fresh herbs, double the amounts called for.

Joyce Fasi's Taste-as-You-Go Tomato Sauce | Appeared Jan. 29, 1989

½ medium onion, chopped (about ¾ cup)	1-2 bay leaves
2 (28-ounce) cans crushed tomatoes	1 teaspoon cayenne pepper
4-6 (8-ounce) cans tomato paste	Pinch of baking soda
2-2½ quarts water	(tames acid in tomato taste)
3-4 cloves garlic, crushed	Olive oil
1 tablespoon dried oregano	2 thick pork chops
2-3 tablespoons dried Italian seasoning mix	2-3 bone-in chicken thighs
1-2 tablespoons anise seeds	1 soup bone
½ tablespoon fennel seed	

In a large (10-quart) kettle, combine crushed tomatoes, tomato paste, water, garlic, seasonings, and baking soda ❖ Bring to a boil over medium heat ❖ Heat olive oil in a large frying pan and brown pork chops and thighs; place in sauce with soup bone ❖ Cover and simmer over low heat for 3 to 4 hours until reduced to two-thirds of a potful ❖ Stir and taste often, adding salt and other seasoning as needed ❖ Before serving, remove soup bone and meats; cut meat from bone and return to sauce; discard bones.

❖ *Serves 12 or more.*

Variations:
*Frank Fasi's Meatballs:
Cook browned, Italian-style meatballs (beef, pork, milk-soaked bread or breadcrumbs, grated cheese) in the sauce for 30 to 45 minutes.

*Frank Fasi's Braciola:
Or make Frank Fasi's favorite, braciola — thin-sliced top round steaks stuffed with a mixture of pork, cheese, and herbs, rolled and skewered or tied with cotton cooking string. Cook in sauce 30 to 45 minutes.

*Or serve sauce over pasta; Frank Fasi's favorite is conchiglioni (shells) because they hold more sauce.

Tip

If a recipe that's to be cooked long and slow calls for minced garlic or grated ginger, save time and trouble by smashing them instead. Smash garlic cloves with the peel on; then peel. Cut or scrape away ginger skin, slice, and then smash. To smash: place on a cutting board, lay the side of a cleaver on cloves or slices a few at a time and give knife a good whack with the side of your fist. The pieces will break apart and "melt" during cooking.

Tip

To skim fat from hot mixtures, use a large, shallow spoon and dip into the fat gently, at an angle. Or wrap an ice cube in a paper towel and swirl it slowly over the surface; the chilled fat will adhere to the towel. Or refrigerate overnight and scrape away fat in the morning.

Short Ribs

The term "short ribs" refers to a family of beef cuts from the 12 ribs between the chuck (shoulder) and the loin. The term's meaning varies around the country. In the Islands, short ribs are often cut for Korean kalbi barbecue; these may be sliced crosswise thick or thin but are always bone-in. Short ribs may also be cut across the bone into chunks. In Hawaiian Short Ribs, I used 1-inch-thick kalbi-cut ribs, but any cut of beef that benefits from long, slow, moist cooking could be substituted.

In 1980, a Honolulu institution, The Willows, changed hands. Many worried that their menu favorites would disappear (and some did, but the restaurant continues to operate in its enchanting garden-and-pond setting in Mōʻiliʻili). Kathleen Perry, a member of the family that had long owned The Willows, shared recipes for several signature dishes, including these short ribs. (Islanders *love* short ribs; there are dozens of recipes for them.) Ample enough for potluck, these can be made a day or two ahead. If making ahead, don't add cornstarch slurry until you reheat the dish.

Hawaiian Short Ribs | Appeared March 26, 1980

1	tablespoon vegetable oil
5	pounds short ribs
½	cup plus ½ cup sherry
1	cup water
1¼	cups brown sugar
1½	cups pineapple juice
1	tablespoon beef base (i.e. Minor's beef broth concentrate or Kitchen Bouquet)
1	finger-length knob of peeled fresh ginger, sliced and smashed
6	cloves garlic, peeled and smashed
¼	cup cider vinegar
1	teaspoon salt

Freshly ground pepper to taste
1   tablespoon cornstarch whisked into 2 tablespoons
         water to make a slurry

In a large Dutch oven or other heavy pot, heat vegetable oil over medium-high heat ❖ Working in batches and not crowding the pieces, brown short ribs on all sides, removing the browned ones to a plate until all are done ❖ Pour off most of the oil ❖ Using a heatproof spatula, scrape up the browned bits and return pan to heat ❖ Deglaze the pot with ½ cup sherry ❖ Return meat to pan and add water, brown sugar, juice, remaining ½ cup sherry, beef base, ginger, garlic, vinegar, and salt and pepper ❖ Bring to a boil; turn down heat and allow to simmer, partly covered, until meat is tender and falling from the bone, 2 hours or more ❖ Skim oil and stir in slurry to thicken.

❖ *Serves 10 to 12.*

For a story on how Islanders celebrate Super Bowl Sunday, the *Advertiser* visited with Wayne and Patti Silva, who each year hold the "Silvadome," a backyard party during which guests can watch the Super Bowl game inside or chat and play games outside. A favorite Silvadome dish is this ultra-simple barbecued pork from the Philippines, in which the pork slices are steeped in the complex and pungent flavor of fish sauce, barbecued, and served topped with a tomato-and-onion salad. A splash of calamansi juice would finish this off nicely; lime juice is an acceptable substitute.

Calamansi

Calamansi (kah-lah-mahn-SEE), Philippine lime, is a golf ball–size green-to-orange citrus fruit available in farmers' markets in the Islands. It's often splashed on Philippine salads and other dishes as a final bit of flavor polish. The juice can be purchased in vacuum pouches online at www.yollieoriental.com.

Philippine Barbecued Pork | Appeared Jan. 23, 1991

2-3 pounds boneless Boston Butt
1 cup patis (Philippine-style fish sauce)
¼ teaspoon finely ground black pepper
2 cloves garlic, crushed and minced
2 firm tomatoes, finely diced
1 small sweet onion, finely diced

Slice pork into ½-inch slices; place in container with lid and pour patis over, then sprinkle with black pepper and minced garlic ✤ Cover, refrigerate, and marinate for 1 hour ✤ Barbecue over hot coals until pork is very well done ✤ Slice into bite-size pieces, mix with tomatoes and onions and place on a serving plate ✤ Serve with toothpicks as a *pūpū*, or over hot rice as an entrée.

✤ *Serves 6 as an entrée, 12 as an appetizer.*

This casserole defines holiday gatherings for the sprawling family of Joan Dowsett Osborne of Kailua (she's the mother of 4 and grandmother and great grandmother of too many to count). Osborne got the casserole from a woman with whom she once worked, and it makes two huge baking dishes, enough to serve a large and hungry crowd. It's best when piping hot.

Liz Elliott's Casserole | Appeared Nov. 10, 2004

6 pounds hamburger
6 tablespoons butter
6 cloves garlic, minced
24 ounces tomato sauce
   (or canned diced tomatoes)
2 teaspoons salt
3 teaspoons sugar

1 teaspoon pepper
7 cups farfalle (bow tie pasta)
1½ cups sliced green onions
3 (8-ounce) blocks cream cheese
3 (16-ounce) cartons sour cream
1½ cups grated Cheddar cheese
Paprika

Preheat oven to 350 degrees ✤ In a large frying pan, brown hamburger in butter; drain fat ✤ Add garlic, tomato sauce, salt, sugar, and pepper ✤ Meanwhile, cook pasta according to package directions ✤ Drain ✤ In a large bowl, mix together green onions, cream cheese, and sour cream ✤ Butter 2 (9 x 13–inch) baking dishes ✤ In two layers, layer meat, noodles, and cream cheese mixture with one-third of Cheddar ✤ Top with remaining one-third Cheddar and sprinkle with paprika ✤ Bake for 25 to 30 minutes, until bubbling hot.

✤ *Serves 25 to 30.*

The late Kinau Wilder was a well-known artist, socialite, and actress who often made this casserole for the cast and crew of community theater productions. It was called "More" for an obvious reason: people always wanted seconds. In 1958, she told an *Advertiser* reporter that, in those days, the dish cost about $5 and was enough for a dozen people.

Kinau Wilder's More | Appeared Aug. 9, 1958

1   pound hamburger
2-3 large onions, sliced
12   ounces shell macaroni
1   tablespoon dry mustard
1   (4-ounce) jar chopped pimientos
1   (5¼-6-ounce) can ripe pitted olives
1   (14.5-ounce) can tomato soup
1   (8-ounce) can tomato sauce
1   (15.5-ounce) can creamed corn
1   (10-ounce) package frozen peas
Salt and pepper to taste
Garlic to taste
Worcestershire sauce to taste
Paprika to taste

Preheat oven to 325 degrees ✤ In a frying pan, brown hamburger and drain all but a little of the fat ✤ Brown onions in remaining fat ✤ Cook macaroni according to package directions ✤ In a large bowl, mix together hamburger, onions, and macaroni and add mustard, pimientos, olives, soup, sauce, corn, and peas ✤ Season to taste with the spices, garlic, and Worcestershire sauce ✤ Place in a buttered 9 x 13–inch baking dish ✤ Bake for 30 to 40 minutes ✤ May be prepared in advance and frozen.

✤ *Serves 12 or more.*

Loosely based on several recipes, including one in a 1987 *Advertiser* food page story on "Picnicking the Island Way," and another shared by my cooking pal, *Advertiser* promotions director Darilyn Fernandez, this is one of a large family of packed rice casseroles made by Islanders. They are rooted in the Japanese tradition of sushi and *musubi*.

 Potluck Layered Rice | From Wanda's Kitchen

- 8 cups freshly steamed hot Japanese-style short-grain rice
- 2-3 cups mayonnaise or Thousand Island dressing
- 4 cups fresh steamed crab or 5 (6-ounce) cans oil-packed tuna, drained
- 3 ripe avocados, pitted and thinly sliced
- ¾ cup diced *takuwan* (Japanese pickled radish; see Note; optional)
- 5 Japanese or English cucumbers, peeled, seeded, and finely grated

  Furikake (Japanese seasoning; see page 33; optional)

> "Rice is going up. It's advanced 25 cents per 100 pounds wholesale. The increase hasn't affected the housewife yet."
>
> — Jan. 19, 1923

Line a disposable 9 x 13–inch potluck pan with waxed paper ❖ Press half the rice into pan ❖ Spread with mayonnaise ❖ Top mayonnaise with layers of crab or tuna, ripe avocado slices, and *takuwan* ❖ Press remaining rice over the top (you may have some rice left over; don't mound it, keep it flat and leave room for the final layer) ❖ Pack it well so layers stick together ❖ Top with well-drained grated cucumber ❖ Cool and cover with plastic wrap until serving time ❖ To serve, turn onto a flat platter or cutting board, peel off waxed paper and cut into squares.

❖ *Serves 15.*

Note: If you can't get *takuwan*, use crisp pickles — either sweet bread and butter pickles, pickle relish, or chopped dills.

Takuwan

Order *takuwan* online or make it at home. It's a quick fresh pickle that is ready to eat in 24 hours. Peel and cut 2 to 3 large daikons (Japanese white radish) into quartered rounds. Place in sterile jars or in a bowl. Combine 1 cup sugar, ¼ cup white vinegar, 1 cup water, 2 tablespoons salt, and ½ teaspoon yellow food coloring. Pour over daikon. Cover and refrigerate 24 hours. Store in airtight containers up to 1 month.

CHAPTER 3

Daily Grindz

ISLAND-STYLE
ENTRÉES

*E*xcept in certain circles, Hawai'i folk don't go in much for sit-down dinner parties, other than the occasional multicourse Chinese banquet, and those are usually taken in restaurants. Still, even if it's served on a picnic table on the *lānai* while family and friends drop in and drift away, we enjoy a well-made entrée. And we're very open-minded about what that might be. Regardless of the ethnicity of the host, dinner is as likely to be a Thai-style curry as a pot of Hawaiian poi stew. It's equally acceptable to re-create a dish from a high-end restaurant as to bust out Mom's SPAM cakes or corned beef pasties.

"Those wishing to see a sample of Hawaiian beef should step into the store of Chas Brewer 2ND, and examine a lot for sale there. This lot of 200 pounds was packed under the experienced eye of Capt. Jas Makee at his plantation on East Maui."

— Feb. 19, 1857

Beef

In the 1950s and '60s, Swiss steak was a frequent weeknight dinner, a cafeteria lunch standard, and a common diner lunch special. The full-flavored dish of pounded round steak in thick gravy has nothing to do with Switzerland. Technically, its name should be "swissed" steak, because the title refers to a process called swissing, in which fabric, paper, and other textiles are pounded or run through rollers to soften them. Pounding, with a meat hammer or the edge of a heavy saucer, plus long, slow, moist cooking, tenderizes tough round steak (from the hind leg of beef). This is a perfect candidate for the slow-cooker; if using, just add a third more liquid — water, beef broth, or crushed tomatoes.

Swiss Steak | Appeared Feb. 2, 1950

    3-4 pounds beef round steak, cut 1-2 inches thick
    Salt and pepper to taste
    1   cup flour, seasoned with salt and pepper
    ½   cup lard, bacon drippings, butter, or a combination
    2   large onions, sliced
    2   cups canned crushed tomatoes in purée
    1   (14.5-ounce) can beef broth

Season the steak with salt and pepper and place on a well-floured cutting board ❖ Cover with flour and pound with a meat hammer or the edge of a heavy saucer, turning, adding flour, and pounding until all the flour is taken up by the meat and the steaks have been tenderized all over ❖ In a heavy, deep frying pan with a heat-proof handle, or Dutch oven, melt fat and sweat onions over medium heat until limp and translucent ❖ Remove onions and reserve ❖ Over medium-high heat, brown steaks on both sides ❖ Spread onions on top of steaks, pour tomatoes and broth over, cover and cook slowly either on the stovetop or in a 350-degree oven for 2 to 3 hours ❖ Diced peeled potatoes, carrots, or other vegetables may be added in the last half-hour of cooking.

❖ *Serves 6 to 8.*

"The Queen's Hospital has been doing a good deal of research in dietetics and that research has led to adoption of poi as a health food."

— *Jan. 3, 1936*

James Beard Award-winning chef-restaurateur Alan Wong is known for fine dining — sophisticated Hawai'i Regional Cuisine prepared "The Wong Way." But he's also a country boy who recalls lean plantation times and says his mother's plain, Island-style cooking is still the best. He often hosts events at the restaurant that celebrate old-style ethnic foods, recasting them in a contemporary context. This *poi* stew is one he made for a 2006 event at his Pineapple Room restaurant. Buy *poi* online at www.1stluau.com.

Sea beans

Sea beans (*Salicornia virginica*) is a notched, branching sea vegetable with a crunchy texture and the tang of fresh seawater. Well known in Europe and the Pacific Northwest, where it grows naturally along the coastlines, sea beans are being grown hydroponically in an experimental project in brackish water ponds in Kahuku on O'ahu. To reduce the saltiness, blanch sea beans before use in salads, pickles, or as a vegetable side dish. Sea beans are also known as sea asparagus, glasswort, and marsh samphire.

Alan Wong's Poi Stew | Appeared Sept. 6, 2006

2½ pounds beef stew meat, cut into 1-inch chunks
1   pound ripe tomatoes, quartered
2   teaspoons salt
1   teaspoon pepper
2-3 bay leaves
Water or beef stock

2   (16-ounce) packages *poi*
Chile pepper water, to taste
1   cup sliced Hāmākua oyster mushrooms (*Pleurotus eryngii*) or other fresh mushrooms
Salt and pepper to taste

In a large stew pot, combine stew meat, tomatoes, salt, pepper, and bay leaves, and add water or beef stock to cover ❖ Bring to a boil, turn down heat, and simmer for 2 to 3 hours, until beef is tender ❖ Drain, reserving broth ❖ In the same pot, add *poi* and flavor with chile pepper water, mushrooms, and salt and pepper to taste ❖ If mixture is very thick, return some of the broth to the pot — enough to create a gravy texture ❖ Bring to a boil and simmer until mushrooms are tender ❖ Remove bay leaves and garnish each serving with a tablespoon of sea beans, fern shoots, or chopped tomatoes.

❖ *Serves 8.*

This is a riff on the theme of the Japanese fresh-pickled salad called tsukemono, a salty-sweet mixture usually made with thin-sliced cucumbers but also with other vegetables. To give it a Western turn and make it into a summer day entrée, I added thin-sliced steak. Adding more acid and heat gives the dish a Southeast Asian slant.

No Japanese cucumbers? Use English or conventional cucumbers, seeded.

Piquant Asian Beef Salad | From Wanda's Kitchen

2	pounds tender steak
3	Japanese cucumbers
1	teaspoon Hawaiian or kosher salt
1/2	red onion

For the sauce:
1/2	cup soy sauce
1/2	cup sugar
1/2	cup rice or cider vinegar
3	cloves garlic, smashed
	Juice of 2 lemons
	Splash Tabasco Sauce or Island-style chile pepper water
1	small hot red pepper (Hawaiian *nīoi* or Thai bird chile)

4	cups mixed greens
4	tablespoons toasted sesame seeds, ground or crushed

Idea

For a company dinner, garnish roast meats or fish with fried parsley. Wash a large bunch of curly or Italian (flat-leaf) parsley and dry very well (do this in advance). Divide into smaller bunches. Heat a pot of oil to 350 degrees and fry for a few seconds or until crisp; scoop up with a wide, wire mesh strainer. Sprinkle with fresh-ground sea salt. (You can make this a short while in advance and place in an airtight container when cooled.)

— *Appeared Feb. 17, 1982*

Broil steak to rare; place on plate and cover loosely with foil to cool ❖ Peel cucumbers, leaving alternating thin strips of skin on the cucumbers ❖ Slice thinly into rounds ❖ Place in a colander and layer with salt ❖ Allow to drain in sink for 30 minutes ❖ Meanwhile, cut red onion into paper-thin slices and break into crescents.

Make the sauce: In a large container with a lid, combine sauce ingredients, stirring to dissolve sugar ❖ Slice the steak very thinly ❖ Rinse cucumbers in cold water, drain well and pat dry with paper towels, pressing out water ❖ Add cucumbers, onions and steak to sauce and marinate in refrigerator for at least 1 hour but for no more than 8 hours ❖ Arrange on a bed of greens and dust with ground sesame seeds (toast and grind the seeds right before use for best flavor).

❖ *Serves 4.*

With the punched-up flavors of Southeast Asia, but the heft of good old American beef, this salad makes a lunch or supper entrée that even a hearty eater can appreciate.

From Guam to Samoa to Hawai'i, corned beef is a favorite food in the Pacific — likely a hangover from wartime, when canned meats replaced fresh meat, or were introduced to native peoples by the military. Along with SPAM and Vienna sausage, corned beef was the everyday meat of baby boomer childhoods in the Islands. Here, refrigerated roll dough makes it easy to create a rich, fresh-baked turnover. (You may have some leftover filling, which may be scrambled with eggs and onions the next morning.)

Corned Beef Pasties | From Wanda's Kitchen

$1/2$ cup lard, bacon drippings, butter, or a combination
2   tablespoons butter
$3/4$ cup coarsely chopped onion
1   can corned beef, broken up
$1 1/4$ cups peeled, boiled, finely diced potatoes
1-2 tablespoons mayonnaise
Splash of Tabasco Sauce or chile pepper water
$1/4$ teaspoon ground black pepper
2   (8-ounce) packages refrigerated crescent rolls

Preheat oven to 375 degrees ✤ In frying pan, melt butter and sauté onion until limp and translucent ✤ In a medium bowl, toss together onions, corned beef, potatoes, mayonnaise, Tabasco Sauce or chile pepper water and ground black pepper to taste, incorporating well without mashing too much ✤ Break rolls into triangles along serrated lines; lightly unroll , retaining triangular shape ✤ Place $1/4$ cup filling on half the triangles and cover each with a second triangle ✤ Bake on ungreased cookie sheet about 12 minutes, until golden brown.

✤ *Makes 8 pasties, to serve 4.*

Lamb is not particularly popular in the Islands, possibly because during World War II a lot of gamey-tasting mutton was dumped on the market after shepherds were drafted, and many of our parents never wanted to eat it again. But this Asian-accented recipe, named for a beloved feature of New Zealand's landscape, Mt. Taranaki, made enough of an impression that an *Advertiser* reader wrote to ask for it: "It's the only lamb dish my husband likes," she said.

Lamb Taranaki | Appeared May 31, 2006

2½ pounds leg of lamb (half a leg)
1 bunch green onions, trimmed of roots and chopped
2 cloves garlic, crushed
½ cup soy sauce
5 tablespoons sugar
2 tablespoons sesame seeds, toasted
2 tablespoons sesame oil
Freshly ground pepper to taste

Rinse lamb, pat dry, and place in a 3-inch-deep roasting pan ✜ Combine remaining ingredients and pour over lamb; cover with foil and marinate in refrigerator ✜ Preheat oven to 350 degrees ✜ Roast lamb, still covered with foil, for 2½ hours ✜ Remove foil and return lamb to oven for 15 to 20 minutes, until the marinade forms a rich, syrupy gravy ✜ Spoon off extra fat ✜ Thinly slice lamb, following the grain, and serve with sauce spooned over ✜ May be served hot or cold.

✜ *Serves 4.*

Chicken

Chef Fred Hellekes, then at the Hawaiian Regent Hotel, contributed this palate-awakening dish to a story that focused on ways to use Island-grown foods (green onion, ginger, and — before most of the Islands' processors went out of business— chicken). It's Southeast Asian in style and flavor but Western in technique. Much of the work can be done in advance: poaching the chicken, grinding the spices, and combining flavoring ingredients. Once these tasks are accomplished, the dish takes mere minutes to prepare.

Tip

To lighten recipes that call for coconut milk, use light coconut milk or fresh coconut milk (labor-intensive but worth it).

❀ **Ulupi'i Chicken** | Appeared Aug. 23, 1973

4   skinless, boneless chicken breasts, about 1¾-2 pounds

For spice paste:
2   tablespoons chopped green onion
2   tablespoon chopped garlic
2   tablespoons peeled, chopped fresh ginger
1   tablespoon ground coriander
1   tablespoon chile paste
       (i.e. sambal oelek) or seeded and
          chopped fresh hot chile peppers

2   tablespoons soy sauce
2   tablespoons brown sugar
4   tablespoons butter
1   (13.5-ounce) can coconut milk
⅓   cup water
1   cup dry roasted peanuts
Slurry made of 2 tablespoons cornstarch whisked together with 1 tablespoon water
1   cup very lightly steamed fresh spinach (about 1 pound fresh, or 1 bag baby spinach)
½   cup yogurt

In a saucepan, cover chicken with water and poach over medium heat just until chicken turns white, about 15 minutes ❖ Drain, reserving poaching liquid for another use ❖ Slice chicken breasts across the grain, about 5 to 6 slices each ❖ Set aside.

Prepare spice paste: In a Thai-style mortar and pestle, or in a mini food processor, combine and mash or purée green onion, garlic, ginger, coriander and chile paste ❖ Set aside. In a small bowl, combine soy sauce and brown sugar ❖ Set aside.

In a heavy-bottomed pot or Dutch oven, melt butter and sauté chicken until just caramelized; try to keep pieces whole ❖ Add coconut milk, water, and peanuts; bring to a boil and simmer for 10 minutes ❖ Add the spice paste and soy-sugar mixture; stir and simmer 5 minutes. (At this point, you can set the pot aside over very low heat or in a low oven and hold until shortly before serving.) ❖ Stir in cornstarch slurry, simmer briefly to thicken ❖ Arrange cooked spinach in serving platter or on individual plates ❖ Serve chicken over spinach with a dollop of yogurt on top ❖ Garnish with small, red, hot peppers (Hawaiian *nīoi* or Thai bird chiles) or lemon and/or kaffir lime leaves.

❖ *Serves 4 generously.*

Ulupi'i Chicken pairs sautéed chicken breast a rich sauce of coconut milk, ginger, chilies and other heady ingredients, then is topped with a scattering of peanuts.

Like most newspapers, the *Advertiser* dutifully trotted out a report every year celebrating the state's representative (Shoyu Chicken won the national prize for Kiyoko Aoki in 1973; that recipe is in the first *Island Plate* cookbook). Here are a couple of examples.

Barbara Tanabe of Honolulu contributed this Asian fusion version of fried chicken.

Crunchy Chicken Delight | Appeared June 13, 1979

- 1½ teaspoons salt, divided
- ¼ teaspoon pepper
- 12 boned chicken thighs
- 2 cups vegetable oil for deep-frying
- 1 cup flour
- 1 egg, beaten
- ¾ cup ice water
- 1 clove garlic, minced
- 1 cup fine, dry bread crumbs
- 3 tablespoons ketchup
- 2 tablespoons soy sauce
- 1½ tablespoons white or cider vinegar
- 2 teaspoon sugar
- Dash of liquid hot pepper sauce (i.e. Tabasco Sauce)

Fried Chicken Tip

Many Island cooks substitute rice flour (regular rice flour, not sweet or glutinous rice flour) for all or part of the flour or cornstarch in coating chicken before frying. It doesn't absorb liquid readily, promoting crispness.

Sprinkle 1 teaspoon salt and ¼ teaspoon pepper evenly over chicken ❖ In a large frying pan, heat ½ inch oil to 350 degrees ❖ Meanwhile, in a bowl, make batter by whisking together flour, ½ teaspoon salt, egg, water, and garlic ❖ Place bread crumbs in a shallow dish ❖ Dip chicken in batter to coat evenly, then in bread crumbs, rolling to coat ❖ Add chicken to pan, a few pieces at a time, and cook 15 minutes, until golden brown ❖ Remove one piece to test: fork should be inserted in chicken with ease and juices should run clear ❖ Drain cooked chicken on paper towels ❖ In a bowl, make sauce: mix together ketchup, soy sauce, vinegar, sugar, and hot pepper sauce ❖ With a very sharp knife, cut each thigh in 4 pieces. Serve with sauce as a *pūpū* or entrée.

❖ *Serves 4 as entrée, 8 as an appetizer.*

Thalassa Kawachi of Pāhala on the Big Island went the predictable pineapple-coconut-mac nut route with this fried chicken.

Chicken in Paradise | Appeared Feb. 22, 1989

1½ teaspoons garlic salt
1½ teaspoon ground ginger
½ cup chicken broth
½ cup frozen orange juice concentrate, thawed
8 skin-on, bone-in chicken thighs
2 eggs
½ cup cornstarch
½ cup flour

⅓ cup vegetable oil for frying
Paradise Sauce (recipe follows)
2 tablespoons fresh or dried unsweetened shredded coconut
2 tablespoons finely chopped macadamia nuts
Pineapple rings, drained
2 cups hot cooked rice

Preheat oven to 350 degrees ❖ In a medium bowl, combine garlic salt, ginger, broth, and orange juice concentrate ❖ Marinate chicken in this mixture for 1 hour ❖ In another bowl, whisk eggs until well-beaten ❖ In a separate bowl, whisk together cornstarch and flour ❖ In electric frying pan or on stove, heat oil over medium-high heat ❖ Drain chicken and dip in eggs, then roll in flour and cornstarch mixture ❖ Brown chicken on all sides, about 10 minutes ❖ Place chicken skin-side down in large baking dish ❖ Pour Paradise Sauce over chicken ❖ Bake, turning after first 15 minutes ❖ Sprinkle with coconut and macadamia nuts; cook 15 further minutes ❖ Serve on bed of rice and topped with pineapple rings.

❖ Serves 4.

Variation:
Broil the pineapple rings or sauté them in a little butter before garnishing chicken.

Paradise Sauce

¾ cup loosely packed brown sugar
6 tablespoons finely chopped macadamia nuts
½ cup cider vinegar
½ cup chicken broth
2 tablespoons honey
¼ cup ketchup
1 cup crushed pineapple with liquid

In a medium saucepan, mix together all ingredients ❖ Place over medium heat and cook, stirring until liquid dissolves.

Cleverly named Terrence's Most Excellent Chicken was a finalist in a My Best Recipe competition in 1992. After judging the competition, I couldn't wait to get home and try it. The recipe employs a common Chinese technique: "breading" meat or fish with egg white and cornstarch. To avoid over-breading, use a small strainer to sift the cornstarch over the chicken pieces.

❄ Terrence's Most Excellent Chicken | Appeared Nov. 1, 1992

½ cup lard, bacon drippings, butter, or a combination
2 pounds boneless chicken thighs, cut into bite-size pieces
2 egg whites
2 tablespoons cornstarch
Peanut oil for frying
2 teaspoons chopped garlic
3-5 whole small, red chiles
½ cup dry-roasted peanuts
2 tablespoons hoisin sauce
1½ tablespoons black bean sauce
3 tablespoons brown sugar
2 tablespoons shaohsing
   (Chinese rice wine) or dry sherry

In a small bowl, whisk together egg whites and a couple teaspoons of water ❖ Dip chicken pieces in egg white and place on a flat plate ❖ Using a small strainer, shake cornstarch over chicken pieces; turn chicken and repeat ❖ In a frying pan, heat ½ inch of peanut oil over medium-high heat to 350 degrees ❖ Working in batches, deep-fry chicken pieces until golden brown ❖ Drain on paper towels ❖ Pour deep-fry oil into another pot to cool before discarding ❖ Place 2 tablespoons peanut oil in a large sauté pan and heat over medium-high heat; add chopped garlic and chiles ❖ Fry 30 seconds or so ❖ Add peanuts ❖ Fry 20 seconds or so ❖ Stir in hoisin, black bean sauce, brown sugar, and shaohsing or sherry ❖ Stir in reserved chicken ❖ Correct seasonings to taste and serve.

❖ *Serves 4 to 6.*

Black Bean Sauce

Black bean sauce with garlic is a chunky paste made from salted black beans and minced garlic. It's essential to the rich and salty flavor of Terrence's Most Excellent Chicken. In a pinch, use 1 tablespoon preserved black beans and ½ teaspoon minced fresh garlic.

Umani is a homey Japanese-style stew that has dropped from sight but was once inevitable in any Japanese recipe collection in the *Advertiser* and community cookbooks. This one was from Mrs. Takeo Isoshima.

❋ Umani: Japanese Chicken Stew | Appeared Sept. 25, 1952

1   tablespoon butter or vegetable oil
2-2½ pounds bone-in chicken,
      cut into small pieces
1   cup peeled carrots, cut into
      triangular batonnets
1   cup sliced bamboo shoots
      (canned okay)
1   cup sliced mushrooms
      (straw are traditional but button
      or fresh shiitake are fine)
1   cup sliced gobo (burdock root; optional)
2   tablespoons sugar
1   cup soy sauce
½   cup chicken broth
½   cup water
1   cup Chinese peas (optional)

Burdock root (gobo)

Burdock root, or gobo as it is known in Japan, is a thin, round root vegetable, like an anorexic brown carrot, only a foot or more long with an earthy flavor and tender-crisp texture. Scrape or scrub gobo with a stiff brush or scouring pad, boil 10 minutes in liquid to cover (1 part vinegar to 3 parts water). A substitute for gobo in this recipe might be turnips or parsnips.

In large, deep frying pan or Dutch oven, heat butter or vegetable oil over medium-high heat ❖ Brown chicken on all sides ❖ Add carrots and brown 5 minutes ❖ Add bamboo shoots, mushrooms, and gobo and sauté 5 minutes ❖ Meanwhile, in a bowl or measuring cup, combine sugar, soy sauce, chicken broth, and water; stir ❖ Pour over meat and vegetables and cook 20 to 25 minutes, shaking the saucepan up and down occasionally to mix the ingredients ❖ Serve, garnished with Chinese peas.

❖ *Serves 4 to 6.*

Pork

What is it with Islanders and Spam? The squat, round-cornered blocks of processed pork in the colorful cans gained popularity among plantation families in the post-war years. Why is not such a conundrum: Islanders tended to have large families. Spam cost mere pennies and paired well with rice or noodles. Dice a can of Spam, scramble a couple of eggs, throw in some garden vegetables and, with a pot of rice or pan of noodles, you could feed the entire clan.

Here are a couple of Spam ideas old-timers will remember well.
In this one, Spam takes the place of tuna, 'ahi, or corned beef.

Spam Patties | Appeared April 2, 1986

4	stalks green onion, minced	1	can Spam, diced
1/4	small onion, diced	3	eggs, beaten
4	sprigs Italian (flat-leaf) parsley or cilantro, minced	1	tablespoon soy sauce
		1/4	teaspoon finely ground black pepper

In a bowl, combine green onion, onion, parsley, and diced Spam. In a separate bowl, beat eggs; add soy sauce and pepper ❖ Combine egg mixture with Spam mixture ❖ Form into patties ❖ Oil or spray a nonstick frying pan and cook over medium-high heat, turning, until browned on both sides ❖ Serve with hot rice.

❖ *Serves 4 to 6.*

Here, Spam is the poor man's ham.

Baked Spam | Appeared April 2, 1986

1	can Spam		
6	whole cloves		
3	pineapple rings	1/3	cup brown sugar
2	slightly underbaked yams or sweet potatoes, peeled and cut into chunks or thick slices	1	teaspoon vinegar
		1	teaspoon pineapple juice
		1	tablespoon water

Preheat oven to 350 degrees ❖ Butter a baking dish ❖ Place a whole can of Spam on its side in dish and dot with whole cloves ❖ Cover Spam with overlapping pineapple rings ❖ Arrange yams or sweet potatoes around Spam ❖ In a small bowl, mix together brown sugar, vinegar, pineapple juice, and water ❖ Drizzle mixture over Spam, pineapple , and yams or sweet potatoes ❖ Bake 30 to 40 minutes, basting occasionally with pan drippings.

❖ *Serves 3 to 4.*

Though they are a Shanghai specialty, lion's head meatballs are beloved in Hong Kong and are on the banquet menus of Cantonese restaurants. The chef may make one giant meatball, said to resemble the head of a lion with a cabbage mane floating around it. More commonly, medium-size individual meatballs are served one to a customer in bowls with broth and cabbage.

The preferred cabbage for use in this dish is Shanghai cabbage, a miniature leaf cabbage frequently mislabeled baby bok choy; look for light celadon stems. If need be, substitute bok choy, Napa cabbage, or even regular round cabbage. Note the technique for preparing the meat: it is chopped fine rather than ground, then thrown in the bowl to create the desired sticky texture.

❀ Sha Kuo Shih Tzu Tou: Lion's Head Meatballs | Appeared Feb. 6, 2008

For the meatballs:
- $1\frac{2}{3}$ pounds pork (half fatty, half lean)
- 1 egg, beaten
- 1 tablespoon Shaohsing (Chinese rice wine) or dry Sherry
- $1\frac{1}{2}$ tablespoons cornstarch
- $\frac{1}{4}$ teaspoon black pepper
- 1 (1-inch) piece of ginger, finely grated
- 5 green onions, chopped fine
- 3 tablespoons shallots or onions, chopped fine

$1\frac{1}{4}$ pounds Shanghai cabbage (a.k.a. baby bok choy)

For the sauce:
- 1 cup chicken broth
- 4 teaspoons dark soy sauce
- 2 teaspoons all-purpose soy sauce
- 2 teaspoons sugar

Slurry made of 2 tablespoons cornstarch whisked into 4 tablespoons cold water

Preheat oven to 350 degrees ❖ Make the meatballs: Dice the pork and continue chopping until it is a little courser than ground meat ❖ Chinese cooks often use two cleavers simultaneously ❖ Place chopped pork in bowl ❖ Add egg, wine, cornstarch, pepper, ginger, green onions, and shallots ❖ With your hands, stir the meat, revolving always in one direction ❖ Take the meat in one hand and tilt the bowl in the other ❖ Throw the meat vigorously back into the bowl, repeating for several minutes, until pork mixture is very sticky ❖ Working lightly, without overly compressing the mixture, form the meat into about 20 golf ball–size spheres ❖ Line a cookie sheet with silicone baking mat (i.e. Silpat), nonstick foil, or parchment paper ❖ Bake meatballs for 20 minutes ❖ Drain and discard oil.

While the meatballs brown, prepare the cabbage: Bring a large pot of water to a boil ❖ Cut cabbage into 3-inch strips ❖ Fill a bowl with water and ice and set aside ❖ Boil the stems of the cabbage for 1 minute, add the leaves and continue cooking for another minute ❖ Drain the cabbage and immediately plunge into ice water to stop cooking ❖ Drain and set aside.

Make the sauce: In a saucepan, combine sauce ingredients except the slurry ❖ Bring to a boil and cook on medium heat for 5 minutes ❖ Whisk in cornstarch slurry and cook until thickened for one minute ❖ Keep on low.

Assemble dish: Arrange the cabbage in a layer on a decorative platter, family-style in one large casserole, or in individual casseroles ❖ Arrange the meatballs on top of the cabbage and drizzle sauce over ❖ Garnish with green onions ❖ Serve immediately as a second or third course during a festive meal.

❖ *Serves 6 to 8.*

Variant:
To add color and texture: after baking meatballs, dip cooked meatballs in soy sauce and brown under the broiler for 5 minutes or in a frying pan with a little oil.

Most people in Hawai'i think saimin is Japanese. But food historians believe the dish has Chinese roots and was likely heavily influenced by the many Japanese entrepreneurs who founded small noodle shops here and married their ramen tradition with Chinese *sai mihn*. Ramen, Japanese noodle soup, has a pork base in Japan but often a dashi base (fish and seaweed) here and thick udon noodles. *Sai mihn* (meaning "thin noodle" in Cantonese) is made with a pork (or pork and chicken) broth and noodles about the diameter of knitting yarn; there's a slightly fishy background from ingredients such as dried shrimp or abalone and a distinctive saltiness from the fermented mustard greens called *chung choy* (see Chung choy, page 89). Island-style saimin is usually made with dashi and Chinese-style thin noodles. And it's a whole meal, heartily topped with sliced roast meats, hard-boiled eggs, kamaboko (fish cake), omelet strips, and even teriyaki beef or chicken skewers. This recipe makes a delicate broth; the longer you reduce it, the more pronounced the flavor. Some saimin stands simmer the broth overnight.

What are the right noodles for saimin?

Saimin noodles are thin wheat noodles, sold fresh, frozen, or dried in 1-serving coiled blocks Drop fresh noodles into boiling water for just a minute, drain, and add to broth. Frozen or dried noodles need 2 to 3 minutes of boiling. Commercial packaged saimin or ramen products contain a flavor packet, a salty powdered dashi (fish) base.

Lion's Head Meatballs, common on restaurant banquet menus, make an impressive special occasion meal and don't require much skill; the secret is all in the chopping. Be sure to present them on an attractive bed of freshly steamed greens — preferably Shanghai cabbage (aka baby bok choy), since this dish is of Shanghai origin.

❋ Chinese-Style Saimin Broth | From Wanda's Kitchen

4	quarts (16 cups) cold water
10	dried shrimp (*ama ebi*) or 1 flavor packet from a commercial noodle soup
2	pounds meaty pork bones
1	pound chicken wings
1	piece *chung choy* (Chinese preserved mustard cabbage; optional)
1	(1-inch) square trimmed fresh ginger, sliced
3	dried shiitake mushrooms
2	tablespoons Shaohsing (Chinese rice wine) or dry sherry
2	tablespoons soy sauce

In a soup pot, combine water, shrimp, pork bones, chicken, *chung choy*, ginger and mushrooms ❖ Bring to a boil; skim scum, reduce to a simmer over medium heat, and allow to simmer for 2 hours ❖ Add wine and soy sauce and simmer another ½ hour ❖ The broth will be reduced by about one quarter.

❖ *Serves 10 to 12.*

Saimin:
Place hot, drained boiled noodles in warmed bowl; pour simmered broth over noodles; garnish as desired.

Saimin Braised Pork Topping

1	tablespoon vegetable oil	1	star anise
	Boneless pork tenderloin	½	cup mirin
1	cup chopped cabbage or bok choy	½	cup sake
½	cup sliced green onions	½	cup sugar
2	cloves smashed garlic	1	cup soy sauce
4	slices smashed fresh ginger		

In a large, heavy Dutch oven, heat vegetable oil and brown a boneless tenderloin on all sides (cut in half if crosswise, if need be, to fit pot) ❖ Drop in chopped cabbage or bok choy, green onions, garlic, and ginger and cook briefly until cabbage wilts ❖ Add water to cover, simmer, and cook 25 to 30 minutes ❖ Drain liquid (reserve to use for saimin broth, if desired) ❖ Add to the pork, in the same pot, star anise, mirin, sake, sugar, and soy sauce and cook 30 minutes, simmering gently ❖ Turn off heat, allow pork to cool in liquid; transfer to cutting board and cut into slices ❖ Serve over saimin or hot rice.

❖ *Serves 6 to 8.*

— *Contributed by Nate Lum, Jan. 17, 2007*

Saimin noodle soup is the Islands' favorite cheap eat; homemade Chinese-style pork-and-shrimp broth and a topping of braised pork loin and edamame (soybeans) take it to a new level.

Fish and Shellfish

A trip to Venice inspired me to create a version of a Venetian classic that's served everywhere in that other-worldly city. It's called saor (sah-OAR) — fish in an onion marinade, but there are many, many versions. Small, whole fish, such as sardines or smelt, are traditional, but you can use steaks or fillets of any firm-fleshed fish and I think it might even be good with chicken. At a popular *cichetti* spot in the Dorsoduro neighborhood (a wine bar specializing in small dishes eaten standing up), they even make it with shrimp and serve it on toast — divine! Note that the dish marinates overnight — but it's ready to serve the next day, a perfect dish for entertaining.

> **Tip**
>
> The trick with saor is getting the proportions right for the type of fish you're using. The more oily and full-flavored the fish, the less oil and the more vinegar you use. For a lean fish, drizzle in more oil.

Pesce en Saor: Fish in Onion Marinade | Appeared July 18, 2007

1   pound onions (sweet onions such as Maui are recommended)
Extra-virgin olive oil
3-6 tablespoons white vinegar
1   teaspoon sugar
2   pounds whole small fish such as sardines, smelt, or akule (gutted and cleaned), peeled shrimp, or fish fillets such as salmon, *a'u*, *moi*, monchong, or halibut

Flour
Salt and pepper
$\frac{1}{2}$ cup pine nuts
$\frac{3}{4}$ cup raisins or sultanas, simmered briefly in red wine, grappa, brandy, or other liquor (or water or fruit juice, if preferred)
Salt and pepper to taste

The night before: Slice onions into thin crescents ❖ In a Dutch oven or other heavy-bottomed pan, heat a tablespoon or two of olive oil over medium heat and place onions in pan ❖ Slowly cook onions over low heat until translucent and wilted ❖ Add vinegar and sugar and cook until onions are soft, dense, and golden brown, but still retain their shape, about 30 minutes ❖ Dredge cleaned small fish, peeled shrimp, or fish fillets in flour, salt, and pepper ❖ In a sauté pan, heat olive oil over medium-high heat and fry fish until golden brown, turning once ❖ In a casserole, layer fish and onion mixture, scattering pine nuts and raisins over each layer and adding salt and pepper to taste ❖ Refrigerate overnight and bring to room temperature before serving, or reheat.

❖ *Serves 6.*

The Lyon Arboretum, a University of Hawai'i plant research facility tucked at the back of misty green Mānoa Valley, is a peaceful haven minutes from the busy city. In keeping with its educational mission, the Arboretum joined with the Hawaii Herb Association to host a Herb Festival in 1993, when consumers were just beginning to turn from dried to fresh herbs. For this event, chef Nick Sayada paired grilled fish with an herbed tomato vinaigrette. Choose a mild, white-fleshed fish.

Grilled Fish with Tomato Vinaigrette | Appeared April 8, 1993

    2   tablespoons mixed finely chopped fresh marjoram and thyme, finely chopped
    1/4 cup olive oil
    4   (6- to 8-ounce) fish fillets
    1   cup Tomato Vinaigrette (recipe follows)

In a small bowl, mix together herbs and olive oil ❖ Rub over fish fillets and marinate 30 minutes in a flat, covered container ❖ Heat grill and place fish on the grill, cooking 5 minutes per side (thick fillets may take a little longer) ❖ Place fish on warm plates and spoon Tomato Vinaigrette over.

❖ *Serves 4.*

Tomato Vinaigrette

    1   cup peeled, seeded, and chopped fresh ripe tomatoes
    1/4 cup mixed, minced fresh herbs (marjoram, tarragon, thyme, Italian parsley, and chives)
    1/4 cup lemon juice
    3   tablespoons peeled minced shallots
    1/2 cup fruity-flavored extra-virgin olive oil

In a bowl, combine tomatoes with mixed, minced fresh herbs ❖ Add lemon juice, shallots, and olive oil ❖ Stir briefly.

❖ *Makes 1 1/2 to 2 cups.*

When a restaurant in Texas declined to give her the recipe for a shrimp dish she enjoyed, military wife and nutritionist Prudence Lezy spent several years experimenting to replicate it and came up with the following company dish, which won a 1990 first-place award in the *Advertiser's* long-running "My Best Recipe" contest. It may be served as a first course, in individual ramekins, or as an entrée with pasta.

Shrimp Lezy | Appeared April 4, 1990

16 jumbo shrimp (about 1 pound), peeled and deveined, tail-on
1 cup half-and-half or light cream

For the sauce:
Juice of ½ lemon (about 1½ tablespoons)
1 egg yolk
¼ teaspoon ground white pepper
½ teaspoon salt
2 cloves garlic, peeled and minced
8 tablespoons chilled butter, cut into bits
1 tablespoon minced Italian (flat-leaf) parsley
1 tablespoon minced chives

1 cup flour
1 cup vegetable oil
2 tablespoons grated Parmesan
Parsley sprigs

Butterfly shrimp by slitting along vein cavity without cutting through ❖ Gently spread shrimp open and place in bowl ❖ Pour cream over and refrigerate for 30 minutes, stirring occasionally.

Meanwhile, make sauce: In a small, heavy-bottomed saucepan, whisk together lemon juice, egg yolk, pepper, salt, and garlic ❖ Add half the chilled butter ❖ Place over medium-low heat and stir until butter is melted ❖ Add remaining butter and whisk briskly over low heat until butter is incorporated and slightly thickened ❖ Remove from heat and stir in parsley and chives ❖ Set aside.

Drain shrimp and discard cream ❖ Place the flour in a paper bag and place shrimp inside; shake well to coat shrimp with flour ❖ In a large skillet, over medium-high heat, heat oil ❖ Arrange shrimp, open side down, and sauté for 5 minutes ❖ Do not turn shrimp ❖ Remove, drain briefly on paper towels and arrange in baking dish ❖ Preheat broiler ❖ Place under preheated broiler and broil 5 minutes or until golden ❖ Pour sauce over shrimp, sprinkle with grated Parmesan and run under broiler briefly to melt cheese ❖ Garnish with fresh parsley sprigs.

As an entrée for 4, serve shrimp over lightly buttered angel hair pasta with good bread with which to mop up the sauce ❖ To serve 8 as an appetizer, arrange fried shrimp in 8 heatproof ramekins, broil, sprinkle with cheese and broil again; drizzle with sauce ❖ Serve with fingers of garlic bread.

❖ *Serves 4 as an entrée or 8 as an appetizer.*

"Mullet steamed in ti leaves, all the juice and flavor intact. The luscious surprise of a laulau. A sweet potato right in the hand, the way you WANT to eat it, and tasting so much better that way. Lomi-lomi salmon, with taste and imagination massaged right into it. The wonderful little opihi, flavor unique among shellfish. Roasted kukui nut, ground to a crumbly paste, my favorite flavor-treat of all. The revelation of Hawaiian salt… You live with this food; it's right in your back yard and it's vitamin- and protein-packed. Do you make the most of it?"

— *Food editor, Alice C. Lake, Oct. 9, 1952*

This dish isn't pretty but it is both easy to prepare and surprisingly delicious. And it's one of the few times when iceberg lettuce is the preferred choice; unlike leaf lettuce, the thickish leaves retain a bit of crisp texture and absorb the lemony fish juices. A little butter adds some richness but the dish works well without it. And even the mayonnaise relish, an alternative to conventional tartar sauce, isn't necessary if you're counting fat and calories.

Fish in Lettuce Leaves | Appeared July 27, 1971

$1/2$ head iceberg lettuce
$1 1/2$-2 pounds *mahi mahi* fillets or other white-fleshed fish
$1/8$ cup lemon juice (juice of $1/2$ lemon)
$1/4$ teaspoon Hawaiian or kosher salt
Dash white pepper
2 tablespoons cold butter, cut into
  small chunks (optional)
Mayonnaise-Pickle Relish (recipe follows)

Preheat oven to 350 degrees ❖ Wash iceberg lettuce, separating into individual leaves; do not dry ❖ Line a baking dish with half the wet lettuce leaves ❖ Lay the fish fillets on the leaves ❖ Drizzle lemon juice and sprinkle salt and pepper over fish ❖ Dot with knobs of butter, if using ❖ Cover with remaining lettuce leaves, tucking them into the sides of the baking dish ❖ Bake fish for 25 to 30 minutes, until internal temperature reaches 130 degrees on an instant-read thermometer (fish will continue to cook when removed from oven) ❖ Before serving fish, tilt serving dish to one side and spoon liquid over lettuce on top ❖ With a sharp knife, cut lettuce-covered fish into serving pieces and serve, spooning more liquid over ❖ Serve with mayonnaise-pickle relish to drizzle over, as desired.

❖ *Serves 4.*

Mayonnaise-Pickle Relish

⅓ cup Homemade Mayonnaise made with coarse Dijon mustard (see page 10)
2 tablespoons finely chopped cornichon pickles, drained
Freshly ground pepper to taste

In a small bowl, combine mayonnaise and pickles ❖ Add a little freshly ground pepper ❖ Taste and add more lemon juice or salt, if desired.

Vee Fallon was among winners of an *Advertiser* seafood recipe contest with this creamy crab dish so easy to prepare and yet so lush and unctuous that no one need fear serving it for a company dinner. The recipe may be doubled. If you don't own a double boiler, you can make do with a heatproof bowl set over a pot; be sure the bottom of the bowl does not touch the simmering water, and don't let the water boil, to avoid curdling the mixture.

Vee's Treasure | Appeared Jan. 24, 1979

1 (8-ounce) package cream cheese
1 (10¾-ounce) can cream of mushroom soup
1 tablespoon soy sauce
2 large, fresh mushrooms, wiped clean and cut into bite-size chunks
4 tablespoons slivered green or red bell pepper (or a mixture of colors)
1 cup chopped carrots
1 cup frozen peas
1 cup fresh, frozen or canned corn kernels
1 pound fresh crabmeat (see Note)

Place 3 cups of water in the bottom of a double boiler ❖ Bring water to a simmer but not a full boil ❖ In the top of the double boiler placed over the simmering water, combine cream cheese, soup, and soy sauce ❖ Stir until well-blended ❖ Add remaining ingredients and stir until well-mixed and warmed through ❖ Turn into container with cover and refrigerate for 24 hours.

Shortly before serving, again heat 3 cups water in the bottom of a double boiler ❖ Bring water to a simmer and place crab mixture in top of double boiler ❖ Heat 15 minutes, stirring occasionally ❖ Serve immediately over 3 cups steamed white or brown rice ❖ Garnish with a few tablespoons of crispy chow mein noodles.

❖ *Serves 3 to 4.*

Note: Frozen lump crabmeat, thawed, works well in this dish and means less work.

Jhun are Korean pan-fried cakes made with meat, fish, and even vegetables dipped in an egg batter. Many U.S. soldiers who served in South Korea came back with a taste for *jhun* and it's a popular choice in the Islands' many Korean barbecue spots. This recipe was contributed to a seafood recipe competition by Mrs. Clarence B. S. Choi.

 Shrimp Jhun | Appeared Jan. 24, 1979

For the sauce:
- 3   tablespoons soy sauce
- 3   tablespoons white vinegar
- 2   teaspoons sesame seeds, toasted and crushed
- 1   teaspoon chopped green onions
- 1   hot green chili pepper, cut in half and seeded (optional)

Dash of ground black pepper

For the shrimp cakes:
- 1   pound uncooked large shrimp (thawed and drained, if frozen)
- 3   tablespoons soy sauce
- 1   teaspoon sesame oil
- 1   teaspoon honey
- 2   teaspoons sesame seeds, toasted and ground (in a mortar and pestle)
- 1   stalk green onion, chopped fine
- 1   clove garlic, crushed

Vegetable oil for frying
- 1   cup or more of flour
- 3   eggs

Salt and black pepper

In a medium bowl or storage container, combine sauce ingredients and set aside.

Peel shrimp, devein, butterfly, and flatten by whacking them with the back of a knife or cleaver ❖ In a flat baking dish, combine soy sauce, sesame oil, honey, sesame seeds, green onion, and garlic ❖ Place shrimp in this marinade for 30 minutes.

Place oil in medium-size frying pan to a depth of ¼ inch ❖ Heat over medium-high heat until a little flour thrown into the hot oil sizzles ❖ Drain shrimp of marinade ❖ Place flour on a flat plate ❖ Beat eggs with salt and pepper to taste in a shallow bowl ❖ Dredge shrimp in flour and then in egg ❖ Fry shrimp in oil until golden brown ❖ Drain on paper towels.

Serve hot with hot rice or cut into bite-size portions and serve as an appetizer ❖ Pass sauce for guests to drizzle on the shrimp *jhun*.

❖ *Serves 4 as an entrée with rice and 6 as an appetizer.*

Mixed Grill

Pan-roasting is a technique often employed by chefs but rarely by home cooks. A demonstration by chef Traci Des Jardins of San Francisco's Jardinière inspired me to learn pan-roasting. Now it's a standard in my kitchen because it allows you to do other things while the dish finishes in the oven. The technique caramelizes the exterior of the meat or fish while the inside remains moist. It's important to use a thick cut of meat or fish; thin cuts overcook easily. Choose ingredients that can stand up to handling: well-marbled beef steaks; skin-on, bone-in chicken; Kurobuta pork chops; 'ahi steaks or swordfish. Seasoning can be as simple as salt or pepper or as complex as you like. (My fallback is the Gourmet Seasoning from Ali'i Kula Lavender on Maui; it's killer.)

Pan-Roasted Whatever | From Wanda's Kitchen

2-3 pounds thick-cut beef, pork, fish, or chicken, in 3- to 5-ounce fillets, steaks
    or chops bone-in or boneless
Salt, pepper or other spices, as desired
1-2 tablespoons of canola or grape seed oil; or 3 parts oil, 1 part butter
1   tablespoon chilled butter for finishing

Rub or sprinkle beef, pork, fish, or chicken generously with salt and pepper or other spice mixture
❖ Preheat oven 350 degrees ❖ Place oil or oil-butter mixture in heavy frying pan with heatproof handle; heat to medium-high ❖ Lay meat or fish in pan (skin-side down, if it has skin) ❖ Sear for 6 to 8 minutes, until nicely browned ❖ Turn and sear 8 to 10 minutes ❖ Place in oven and finish, roasting for 10 to 12 minutes until cooked through. (Check doneness with instant-read thermometer.)
❖ If desired, place a thin slice of cold butter, or an herbed butter mixture, on each ❖ If the primary ingredient is meat or chicken, cover loosely with foil and set aside for a few minutes, to allow juices that have boiled to the surface to be reabsorbed by the meat ❖ Fish should be served promptly.

❖ *Serves 4.*

Tip: For pan-roasting

- Use heavy frying pan with a heatproof handle
  (cast iron, copper, or stainless)
- Do not use a nonstick pan
- Use oil (canola or grape seed); part butter is okay
- Don't crowd ingredients in pan
- Begin skin-side down; then turn
- Season ingredients generously
- Fillets, chops, or steaks should be of even thickness
- Cooking times vary; fish needs less time than meat or chicken
- Use an instant-read thermometer to assure doneness

Pan-roasting steaks, chops and fillets takes just minutes of hands-on work, lends itself to almost any culinary theme from Italian to Indian and gives the cook time to tend to other matters while the meat or fish finishes.

Vegetarian

This portable stuffed sandwich — featured in a story about a cooking class by San Francisco cooking school proprietor (and well-known political activist) Peter Jacobs — is perfect picnic food. The sandwich is prepared in advance and the flavors allowed to meld overnight; the vegetables marinate in the dressing while delicately flavoring the bread. It's like a deli in a sandwich, but light and vegetarian.

Patafla | Appeared Feb. 27, 1971

1   sourdough French bread loaf or three (6-inch) mini-baguettes, sliced lengthwise
3   tomatoes, diced ½ inch square, drained
5   Spanish olives, sliced
5   black olives, sliced
Half a medium onion, finely chopped
3   green onions, finely chopped
2   tablespoons capers, drained
2   tablespoons sweet gherkins or pickles, drained and chopped
Half a bell pepper in thin slivers (any color)

For the dressing:
4   tablespoons olive oil
1   tablespoon balsamic vinegar
1   teaspoon paprika
Salt and pepper to taste

With a spoon, scrape out the soft bread center without breaking through the crust or leaving it too thin ✤ Reserve both bread and crust ✤ Drain all the vegetables on paper towels and pat dry lightly to absorb excess juice ✤ While the vegetables are draining, make the dressing; whisk together all ingredients in a small bowl ✤ Set aside ✤ In a medium bowl, lightly toss together drained vegetables, soft bread, and dressing ✤ Mix thoroughly and add a little salt and pepper to taste ✤ Stuff this mixture into the bottom half of the loaf or baguettes ✤ Mound the filling while pushing down gently to compress ✤ Put the bread halves back together ✤ Wrap tightly in foil and then place in a zippered plastic bag ✤ Refrigerate overnight. When ready to serve, remove from refrigerator and carefully cut into 1-inch slices.

✤ *Makes 18 slices, to serve 6.*

CHAPTER 4

Siders

SOUPS, STARCHES, SALADS, AND VEGETABLES

I can't tell you how many times this carb addict has walked out the door
humming about the salad or side dish. And when you're having company, a side can be easier to pull off than
a mind-blowing entrée or dessert — a fabulous first-course salad (served when everyone is at their hungriest)
or a life-changing risotto can disguise the fact that all you did was grill a steak or poach a piece of fish and throw
together some good ice cream and fruit for dessert.

Caesar salad is one of those dishes about which there is endless debate: how and where it originated, the proper
techniques and ingredients for making one. In 1972, retired Sports Illustrated writer Robert W. Johnson gave
his version of the story, and the salad recipe, in a diatribe headlined "But There Is Only One Honest-to-Goodness
Caesar!" Johnson said he knew this for a fact, having first tasted the salad in 1947: the inventor, he claimed
was Caesar Cardini, at Caesar's Hotel, on the corner of 5TH and Revolucíon in Tijuana, Mexico. "Some day
break a trip to California with a side trip to Tijuana. Park your car on the north side of the border and take
a cab ($2) to Caesar's Hotel."

Caesar Salad | Appeared Nov. 9, 1972

3 medium heads romaine lettuce	Juice of 1 lemon
1 clove garlic, pressed	1 tablespoon wine vinegar
⅔ cup extra-virgin olive oil	Dash Worcestershire sauce
Salt	5-6 tablespoons grated Parmesan
Freshly ground pepper	1 cup toasted croutons
1 egg	

One hour before serving, separate lettuce leaves, wash, dry thoroughly, and chill, wrapped in paper
towels ❖ Crush garlic into olive oil and allow to marinate at room temperature ❖ At table, place
the lettuce in a large salad bowl ❖ Add salt, pepper, and garlic-oil ❖ Toss ❖ Break egg into salad and
douse with lemon juice, wine vinegar, and Worcestershire sauce (this seems to have a marinating
effect) ❖ Toss salad again thoroughly ❖ Add cheese and croutons ❖ Toss again lightly.

❖ *Serves 4.*

For a weekend lunch for friends, or a light supper when it's just too hot to eat, this Thai-style fish salad, contributed to an *Advertiser* recipe competition by Sylvia Meyer, is one flavorful answer. With no oil in the recipe, this one is kind to the waistline. (I tested this with halibut, in season, and it was lovely.)

 Hot Thai Fish Salad | Appeared Jan. 24, 1979

> ½ pound wahoo (*ono*) or other white-fleshed fish, in thick fillets
> 2 medium Japanese or English cucumbers
> ½ sweet or red onion (or less, to taste)
> 2-3 Thai bird chile peppers
> Juice of 3-4 fresh limes
> Salt and pepper to taste
> ½ bunch torn fresh mint

Poach fish on a rack over gently simmering water ✢ Cool; flake or cut into bite-size pieces ✢ Peel cucumbers, leaving alternating thin strips of skin ✢ Cut lengthwise into 4 pieces and slice thinly ✢ Slice onion very thinly and break into segments ✢ Seed chile peppers and chop very fine ✢ In a salad bowl or on a serving platter, combine fish, cucumbers, onions, and peppers ✢ Squeeze lime juice over all and toss lightly ✢ Chill ✢ Just before serving, taste, add salt, pepper, and additional fresh lime juice, if desired ✢ Garnish with mint.

✢ *Serves 4.*

Variation:
Make the salad with good-quality water-packed tuna or mackerel. Add a drizzle of oil — vegetable or sesame — for a little more richness.

Idea

Make "Indian" salad dressing by blending equal parts Thousand Island dressing and mango chutney.

Hawaiian Red Peppers (*nīoi*)

If you can't find Hawaiian red peppers (*nīoi*) or Thai bird chiles, use fresh jalapeños or substitute a dash or two of dried crushed red pepper or ground red pepper sauce.

This salad was born on an evening when I was rooting around in the fridge, craving something lighter, but finding no greens of any kind. I did have a number of other vegetables and some leftover Spanish (pimiento-stuffed) olives so I made a sort of "chop" salad. It tasted so good, it needed no dressing. The olives are the key: they offer oil and richness. The colors give the recipe its name.

Stained-Glass Salad | From Wanda's Kitchen

    1   carrot, peeled and cut into large dice
    1/3 green pepper, seeded and cut into large dice
    1/3 yellow pepper, seeded and cut into large dice
    1   cup cherry, plum, or grape tomatoes, or heirloom tomatoes cut into eighths
    20   whole, seeded olives (pimiento-stuffed or kalamata)
    2   tablespoons minced fresh Italian (flat-leaf) parsley
    1   cucumber, peeled and sliced in rounds
    2   tablespoons red onion or shallots, minced
         Lemon juice
         Salt and pepper
         Lettuce leaves (optional)

In a large bowl, lightly toss together solid ingredients ❖ Add 1 tablespoon lemon juice and a good crank or two of freshly ground pepper ❖ Taste and add additional lemon, salt, or pepper, if desired ❖ Can be served as a dinner salad with grilled or poached chicken or fish, and chunks of feta or goat cheese.

❖ *Serves 4 as a first course, 2 as a dinner salad.*

The only oil in this quick, chop salad is contained in the Spanish olives, which offer just enough bright flavor to elevate this simple dish to company status.

Here's a salad inspired by one I had at a local restaurant. The dish featured Big Island hearts of palm so fresh that they were tender-crisp and subtly sweet — neither woody, as some fresh hearts of palm can be, nor mushy, as the canned or jarred hearts too often are.

Shape can make a big difference in what food scientists call "mouth feel." Julienned vegetables, used here, expose more surface to effectively carry dressings or marinades and while crunching pleasantly.

> "In the suburb of Kalihi, the Alexander Young Hotel maintains a farm of the best, carefully tended produce."
> — Jan. 1, 1904

Crisp Walnut–Hearts of Palm Salad | Appeared March 26, 2008

1/2 bunch leaf lettuce
1/2 English or Japanese cucumber, peeled and cut into matchsticks
1/3-1/2 tender young carrot, peeled and cut into matchsticks
1/3 cup slivered hearts of palm (optional; if available)
1   firm but ripe pear or apple, unpeeled, cored, and cut into matchsticks
Juice of 1 lemon (about 2 tablespoons)
1-2 tablespoons walnut oil
Salt and pepper
3   ounces walnuts

Wash and dry lettuce ❖ Place in zippered plastic bag lined with paper towel; refrigerate ❖ In a small bowl, combine cucumber, carrot, hearts of palm, and pear or apple ❖ Drizzle with lemon juice and walnut oil and flavor liberally with salt and pepper ❖ Cover with plastic wrap; marinate at least 15 minutes ❖ If preparing in advance, chill in refrigerator.

Toast walnuts: bake at 350 degrees or toss and stir in a dry frying pan over medium-high heat until walnuts release fragrance and begin to darken ❖ Rub walnuts in kitchen towel to remove skins ❖ Chop nut meats roughly and set aside.

Just before serving, place lettuce in a bowl, and again season with walnut oil, salt, and pepper ❖ Place marinated vegetables over a bed of greens and allow dressing to drizzle into greens or toss together ❖ Correct seasonings to taste and serve ❖ (If not particularly flavorful or a bit acidic, a sprinkling of sugar or drop of honey or balsamic vinegar can help with the balance.)

❖ *Serves 4 to 6.*

What are hearts of palm?

Hearts of palm are harvested from the shoots of the cabbage palm, a shortish decorative palm tree very unlike our towering coco palms. The outer green stalk is cut away, revealing the white heart, which is cut into short, round lengths. Hearts of palm are at home wherever carrots or celery might be used: cut into strips or coins and served raw in salads, stir-fried or lightly steamed. Trimming away the edible points doesn't kill the tree, so it's a renewable resource. Wailea Agricultural Group (www.waile-aag.com) on the Big Island's Hāmākua Coast has pioneered the industry here, supplying farmers' markets locally and restaurants around the country.

In this healthful salad, hearts of palm, crisp apple or pear, carrots and cucumbers are marinated in a walnut oil mixture that then dresses the bed of greens.

This is a contemporary — and lightened-up — version of a dish that originally included potato chips for crunch and a ton of salad dressing. In testing and lightening the recipe, I was surprised to find that I enjoyed canned salmon — a product I haven't used for years. Just be sure to pick out all the bones.

Crunchy Salmon Salad | Appeared Jan. 8, 1942

¼ cup Homemade Mayonnaise (see page 10)
1 (14.5-ounce) can salmon, bones and skin removed
    (or about 12 ounces boneless, skinless poached fresh salmon)
1 stalk celery, finely chopped (about ⅓ cup)
1 tablespoon minced onion (sweet, red, or other)
⅓ cup finely chopped fresh cherry or other tomatoes
⅓ cup finely chopped cornichon pickles
    (or sweet or kosher pickles depending on your taste)
Lettuce
1 teaspoon butter
2 slices whole grain bread, ground or chopped into coarse crumbs

Lightly toss together mayonnaise and salmon; chill ❖ Add celery, onion, tomatoes, and pickles to salmon mixture; lightly toss ❖ Chill, covered, up to 2 days ❖ Wash and pat or spin-dry leaf lettuce (a half bunch or so) ❖ Line serving platter or individual plates with lettuce ❖ In a sauté pan, melt butter; toss in bread crumbs and fry, stirring frequently, until crumbs are golden brown and butter has been absorbed ❖ On a platter or individual plates, spread lettuce leaves, top with a mound of salmon mixture and garnish with toasted bread crumbs.

❖ *Serves 4.*

Elsie Ching of ʻĀina Haina, a one-time recipe demonstrator for the Extension Service, is my source of all wisdom on Chinese food. But when I visited to learn more about gau (Chinese New Year's sweet rice pudding), she made this very non-Chinese recipe for lunch, one she learned to make from a Portuguese auntie. It seems to have deep roots: the recipe below, which closely resembles Elsie's auntie's recipe, was excerpted from one of the Islands' first cookbooks, the *Central Union Church Cookbook*, published in 1896. It found new life in the *Advertiser* during World War II, when lima beans, onions, and cabbage were among the few readily available vegetables.

Dried Lima Bean Soup | Appeared March 11, 1943

1½ pounds dried lima beans
1¼ pounds smoked ham hocks
    or ham bones or beef soup bones
8 cups water
1-2 large onions

1½ pounds cabbage
1 (8-ounce) can tomato sauce
Salt and pepper
Minced Italian (flat-leaf) parsley for garnish

Soak beans in water to cover overnight ✣ Place in soup pot with soup bones and 8 cups water ✣ Bring to a boil, skim scum, and turn heat down to medium ✣ Simmer 2 hours ✣ Add onions, cabbage, and tomato sauce and cook 30 to 45 minutes, until vegetables are softened but not overcooked ✣ Taste and season with salt and pepper, as desired ✣ Garnish with parsley.

✣ *Serves 8.*

In wartime, wrote *Advertiser* columnist Miriam Jackson Emery, "the preparation of lunch boxes for working members of the family is a new responsibility that has been added to the work of the homemaker." She recommended sending along a thermos bottle of this soup.

Marie's Potato Soup | Appeared Jan. 22, 1942

4	tablespoons butter (or butter substitute)
8	medium onions, peeled and thinly sliced
2	teaspoons sugar
8	medium-sized potatoes
1	(14.5-ounce) can solid-pack (chopped) tomatoes
	Salt and pepper
5	cups boiling water
	Salt and pepper
1	cup "top milk" (light cream) or evaporated milk

In a large heavy-bottomed saucepan or soup kettle, melt butter ✣ Add onions and sprinkle with sugar; cook very slowly until fully caramelized — limp, translucent, and golden brown ✣ This will take 45 minutes to 1 hour; don't rush it ✣ Meanwhile, peel and slice potatoes ✣ When onions are done, add tomatoes, salt, pepper, and potatoes ✣ Add boiling water and simmer until potatoes are fully cooked and soft ✣ Purée in blender or put through a food mill ✣ Correct seasonings to taste ✣ Return to pan, heat to simmering, and add cream or evaporated milk; heat through and serve.

✣ *Makes 4 quarts, to serve about 8.*

Variation:
For more texture, omit the puréeing step. To lighten soup, omit cream or use nonfat whipping cream.

"Before the outbreak of the war, most of the good, red Irish potatoes grown in Hawaii were eaten by Mainlanders who bought them at high prices in Mainland markets. Meanwhile, Island consumers ate Mainland potatoes. This year, our Island potatoes are staying at home."

— *University of Hawaii Home Making Helps, March 18, 1943*

Cooking clubs were a popular '80s phenomenon, with couples preparing elaborate gourmet meals together. A story on one such group in Honolulu included this recipe from Paul and Carol Weaver, who got it from the Franconia Inn in New Hampshire. It's just right as a starter for a meal on a warm evening. Make your own broth or use one of the high-quality organic, vacuum-packed boxed broths.

Cold Tomato Consommé | Appeared Feb. 25, 1980

½ cup lard, bacon drippings, butter, or a combination
3 cups good-quality chicken broth
3 cups good-quality beef broth
2 cups peeled, seeded, chopped very ripe tomatoes
½ cup minced pimiento

2 egg whites, lightly beaten
Crushed shells of 2 eggs (these will clarify the mixture)
Cayenne to taste
2½ tablespoons gelatin
½ cup cold water
Thin lime slice

In a large saucepan, combine the broths, tomatoes, and pimiento ❖ Simmer for 10 minutes ❖ Add the egg whites and crushed shells ❖ Bring to a boil, stirring, and simmer, undisturbed, for 15 minutes ❖ Ladle the mixture through a sieve lined with a rinsed and squeezed cotton kitchen towel or several layers of damp cheesecloth ❖ Season with cayenne to taste ❖ In a small bowl, sprinkle the gelatin over the cold water to soften for 10 minutes ❖ Bring the consommé to a boil and remove pan from heat ❖ Add gelatin and stir until dissolved ❖ Transfer the consommé to a large bowl and let it cool ❖ Chill, covered, until jelled ❖ Divide among chilled cups and garnish with thin slices of lime.

Shep Gordon is a film producer and dedicated foodie who lives on Maui. This recipe was among several shared with *Advertiser* readers in 1989 by his friend chef Roger Dikon, one of the original Hawai'i Regional Cuisine chefs, at that time working in Wailea.

Shep Gordon's Maui Onion and Ginger Soup | Appeared Nov. 1, 1989

2 tablespoons butter
4 large Maui onions, thinly sliced
3 tablespoons peeled and freshly grated ginger
4 sprigs fresh thyme or 1 teaspoon dried

4 cups chicken broth
1 cup white wine
1 cup half-and-half

In a large, deep pot, such as a Dutch oven, melt butter and add onions and ginger ❖ Sauté over medium heat until onions are limp and clear ❖ Add thyme, chicken broth, and wine ❖ Bring to a boil and simmer 30 minutes ❖ Purée in blender, add half-and-half and bring to a boil ❖ Serve hot, or allow to cool and then chill for a warm-weather starter for a company meal.

❖ *Serves 6.*

> **Idea**
>
> Grate peeled ginger into coleslaw.

Tip

To discard oil used in deep frying, allow the used oil to cool somewhat, then fill pot with shredded newspaper or paper towels and allow it to soak up the oil. Discard oily paper in the trash.

> "You will notice that none of the vegetables prepared in Oriental dishes are cooked very soft."
>
> — *Jan. 17, 1930*

Tip

Shanghai-born Linda Chang Wyrgatsch of Pearl City whose gau (Chinese sweet rice pudding) is found elsewhere in this book, uses this trick for avoiding excessive mess when deep-frying. Lay heavy-duty aluminum foil over the top of the stove and any adjacent counter space to catch splatter. For safety, keep foil a couple of inches from the burner you're using.

Chung Choy

Chung choy is salt-preserved Szechuan mustard greens tightly wrapped in highly flavored little bundles, also known as *sin choy*, *harm choy*, and *jar choy*.

Blistered green beans is a favorite restaurant dish in O'ahu's Chinatown. It's usually made with ground pork, but it's equally delicious without meat—though quite rich, so best not indulged in too often.

Blistered Green Beans | Appeared Sept. 28, 2005

1/2	tablespoon dried shrimp or equivalent drained and mashed anchovies (optional)
4	tablespoons shaohsing (Chinese rice wine), dry sherry, sweet vermouth, or other liquor
1	pound yard-long beans or string beans, tips removed
1/4	cup chicken broth
1	tablespoon dark soy sauce
1	tablespoon sesame oil
1	teaspoon minced garlic (1 1/2-2 cloves)
1/4	teaspoon chili sauce (i.e. sambal oelek or garlic chili sauce)
2	cups peanut oil
2	tablespoons *chung choy* (preserved mustard greens), minced (optional)

In a small bowl, immerse dried shrimp in sherry and allow to marinate 1 hour ❖ Wash and dry green beans very well (it's best to do this some time before cooking; lay the beans in a single layer on paper toweling to dry) ❖ In a small bowl, combine chicken broth, soy sauce, sesame oil, garlic, and chili sauce and set aside ❖ Cover a heatproof platter or pan with paper towels ❖ Pour oil into a well-seasoned wok and heat over high heat until a wooden chopstick sizzles when dipped in the oil ❖ Deep-fry the beans in 5 or 6 batches, until they blister and shrivel and turn golden brown in places, 1 to 2 minutes ❖ Use tongs to remove them to the paper-lined platter ❖ Discard all but a couple of teaspoons of oil, place pan over medium-high heat and pour soy sauce mixture into pan along with *chung choy*, if using, and marinated shrimp (with liquid) ❖ Reduce the liquid to a couple of tablespoons, place beans in wok and warm through ❖ Serve immediately.

❖ *Serves 6.*

Variation:
After the beans are blistered and the fat poured off, fry 3/4 pound of ground pork in the oil, breaking up any clumps. Proceed as above.

Blistered Green Beans, a Chinese classic
with or without ground pork, basks in a
soy-based sauce flecked with dried shrimp.
Make it with regular green beans or long beans.

This dish came about because I had just a smidgen of wild rice in the cupboard and wanted to use it up (too expensive to waste, yeah?). I also wanted a vegetable in the dish so I didn't have to prepare a separate vegetable. The short cooking time means the rice remains somewhat crunchy with a full, nutty flavor. I served it under a piece of grilled chicken and it went over big. Feel free to vary ingredients.

Rice Gone Wild | From Wanda's Kitchen

1 tablespoon butter
¼ cup minced parsley
¼ cup minced onion
¼ cup chopped celery or fennel
½ cup corn (raw or frozen) or a
 handful of spinach or other greens

Salt and pepper
¼ teaspoon salt
½ cup wild rice
½ cup long-grain white rice

Melt butter and sauté parsley, onion, and celery or fennel until glazed and tender-crisp; add corn or greens and sauté 1 to 2 minutes ❖ Season with salt and pepper to taste ❖ Set aside ❖ Boil 2 cups water; add ¼ teaspoon salt, wild and long-grain rice, and vegetables; cover and reduce heat to low ❖ Steam 20 to 25 minutes.

❖ *Serves 2 to 4.*

Poi Luncheon Simple

"Do you know that they are very simple to serve and the deviation from an ordinary dinner is quite refreshing? A bit of poi, some fish baked in ti leaves garnished with a chili pepper and a strip of lemon; chicken boiled with taro tops and a little coconut pudding, all of which may be obtained at local market, some of them already prepared."

— *Feb. 17, 1922*

Many don't recall that Hawaiians made *poi* from many things, not just boiled and mashed taro but also bananas and breadfruit, though taro *poi* was their staple food. Sweet potato *poi* pairs well with roast meats, particularly pork or chicken. This recipe was contained in a fascinating 1982 article by *Advertiser* food editor Mary Cooke after she found a few sheets of 40- or 50-year-old, fading, tissue-thin "airmail paper" detailing one Kaua'i hostess' guide to entertaining Island-style.

Sweet Potato Poi | Appeared Feb. 23, 1990

3 cups hot, boiled, riced or mashed peeled sweet potato (see Note)
1½ cups coconut cream (from about 3 coconuts)
1½ tablespoons brown sugar
1 teaspoon salt

Just before serving, combine hot riced or mashed sweet potato with coconut cream, brown sugar, and salt ❖ Consistency should resemble wet mashed potatoes ❖ Serve immediately.

❖ *Serves 6 to 8.*

Note: Ricing is best: forcing the mashed potato through a holed press.

This rapid-fire accompaniment for roast meats or grilled fish came to me one evening when a friend had gifted me with a jar of pesto sauce. You could even serve it over pasta with a good sprinkling of grated Parmesan for a vegetarian supper.

Sautéed Peppers | From Wanda's Kitchen

1 teaspoon olive oil	Generous handful of Italian (flat-leaf) parsley, very coarsely chopped
1 tablespoon butter (optional)	1 tablespoon pesto or a handful of fresh basil leaves
2 cups sliced small sweet peppers of various colors (or seeded, multicolored bell peppers, cut into 1-inch squares)	Salt and pepper to taste

In a sauté pan over medium-high heat, heat together olive oil and butter ❖ Sauté peppers and parsley a few minutes until softened and slightly carmelized ❖ Add pesto or basil, stir, cook for 1 to 2 minutes and serve.

❖ *Serves 4.*

What's coconut cream?

As it was defined in early twentieth-century Hawai'i, coconut cream is the freshly squeezed, creamy milk of grated coconut. Crack the coconut (wrap in a towel and whack sharply with a hammer, aiming at a point along the meridian). When cracked, scrape out the coconut (a toothed coconut grater is helpful for this). Place coconut in a loosely woven cotton flour sack kitchen towel or several layers of cheesecloth and squeeze well, collecting the drippings in a bowl. You need strong hands and persistence for this task. Or take the easy way out: refrigerate several cans of coconut milk; open without shaking and spoon off the thick top cream for use in sweet potato *poi*.

Idea

Bake whole bananas in their skins — place in a baking dish with a little water to prevent sticking (or coat with nonstick spray), bake at 325 degrees until the bananas burst open. Serve in skins; diners cut them open, peel back the skin and eat as is, or pass softened butter and a dish of white or brown sugar for dusting bananas.

Aloo means "potato" in Hindi. I've used it here to describe a dish I made up when I was in the mood for something vaguely Indian and wanted to try out a twice cooked potato cooking technique I saw in a magazine.

Island Aloo | From Wanda's Kitchen

2	pounds new potatoes (red, yellow Finn, or any other small young potatoes)
4	tablespoons ghee, divided
1/4	cup green onion
2	tablespoons garam masala or curry powder
3	cloves garlic, minced
2	tablespoons grated fresh ginger
1/3	cup drained chopped pineapple
6	ounces Greek yogurt or yogurt cheese (see Note)

Salt and pepper to taste

In 1900, Hawai'i's staple starches were, in this order, taro, wheat, rice, and potatoes.

Ghee

Ghee is an Indian form of clarified butter. Purchase it bottled in Indian groceries or make it at home: Place 1 pound unsalted butter in a heavy-bottomed saucepan over medium heat. Raise temperature to medium-high heat, melt butter, and bring to a boil; turn heat down to medium, allowing butter to foam and spit but not brown. Gently push whitish curds aside to look into butter. When the butter is clear (some curds will sink to the bottom), remove from heat and allow to cool to lukewarm. Gently pour the ghee through several layers of cheesecloth into a clean glass jar, leaving curds in pot.

Peel and steam potatoes for 20 minutes, until cooked but still firm; cut into chunks and chill ❖ Preheat oven to 350 degrees ❖ In a bowl, toss together chilled potatoes, 3 tablespoons ghee, green onion, garam masala, garlic, ginger, pineapple, and yogurt ❖ Grease a baking dish with 1 tablespoon ghee and arrange potatoes in it ❖ Bake at 350 degrees for 20 to 25 minutes, until heated through ❖ Serve hot.

❖ *Serves 4 to 6.*

Note: Greek yogurt is plain, natural yogurt that has been drained and allowed to sour slightly; it's tart, rather thick, and smooth-textured. To make yogurt cheese, a similar product, place 1 cup whole milk yogurt with natural cultures in a cheesecloth lined colander, or in a cone-shaped cheese-maker lined with fine-grain plastic screen. Allow to drain overnight. Store in refrigerator.

CHAPTER 5

Sweets and Treats

DESSERTS
AND SNACKS

Desserts

Hunky Bunch mango bread, an O'ahu classic, has a lovely story behind it. The Hunky Bunch (a play on *The Brady Bunch*) was the combined family of the late Dr. Hing Hua "Hunky" Chun and his wife, legislator Connie Chun. They had 6 children from different marriages, who, throughout the '70s, were often seen at fun runs and marathons, usually with a few loaves of mango bread to share with others. If you can't find mango, use canned peaches, well drained.

Hunky Bunch Mango Bread | Appeared Jan. 11, 1984

2	cups flour
2	teaspoons cinnamon
2	teaspoons baking soda
1½	cups sugar
½	teaspoon salt
2	cups fresh mango, diced
1	cup grated fresh coconut
¾	cup salad oil
3	eggs, lightly beaten
½	cup raisins

Preheat oven to 350 degrees ❖ Lightly butter or spray with butter-flavored spray four mini-loaf pans (2½ x 5 inches) or two larger loaf pans ❖ Set aside ❖ In a large bowl, whisk together flour, cinnamon, baking soda, sugar, and salt ❖ Blend in remaining ingredients ❖ Pour batter into pans until two-thirds full ❖ Bake for 55 minutes for small loaf pans or 65 minutes for larger pans ❖ Cool before serving or wrap in foil and freeze.

❖ *Serves 16 to 20.*

For years, caterer Rachel Ige contributed the Okinawan-style holeless donut called *andagi* (ahn-dah-GEE) to a fundraising fair for a local medical center. The deep-fried treats are closer to crullers than cake donuts. The dough is thickish. Serve them hot.

Mrs. Ige's Country Store Andagi | Appeared Oct. 17, 1979

½ inch square, drained	5 medium eggs (4 if eggs are large)
4 cups flour	½ cup evaporated milk
1½ cups sugar (or more, if you like sweeter donuts)	½ cup water
¼ teaspoon salt	½ teaspoon vanilla extract
1 tablespoon baking powder	Vegetable oil for frying

In a large bowl, whisk together flour, sugar, salt, and baking powder ❖ In a medium bowl, blend together eggs, evaporated milk, water, and vanilla ❖ Pour liquid ingredients into flour mixture and mix until the dough forms one big lump ❖ It will be dry and thick, but do not add more liquid ❖ In a large, heavy-bottomed pot or a deep fryer, heat several inches of vegetable oil to 300 degrees ❖ Shape dough into golf ball–size rounds (an ice cream scoop is helpful here) and deep-fry until golden and cooked through ❖ Serve immediately.

❖ *Makes 4 dozen.*

Kabocha (KAH-bow-chah) is a smallish squash that's a Japanese favorite. Simmered in a mild fish broth, chunks of kabocha are a common bar food in Japanese taverns. But cooked and mashed kabocha can be used wherever conventional pumpkin is called for and is much easier to work with because of its size and relative lack of strings and seeds. For a lower-fat Thanksgiving dessert, fill phyllo cups with a no-cook pumpkin mousse. Fill right before serving to avoid soggy dough.

Tip

Kabocha (Japanese for "pumpkin") cooks quickly and conveniently in the microwave. Microwave on High 8 minutes, turn pumpkin over, and microwave 8 more minutes. Allow to cool (it will be so hot when you remove it that escaping steam can burn you if you cut it right away). Cut, scrape out seeds and strings; cut cooked flesh from skin and use as desired. No need to pierce pumpkin; it won't explode!

Kabocha Mousse in Phyllo Cups | Appeared Nov. 23, 2005

For phyllo cups:
   3   sheets phyllo dough, thawed
   Butter-flavored cooking spray

For mousse:
   1   teaspoon 5-spice powder
   ½   teaspoon ground pumpkin pie spice
        (cinnamon, nutmeg, allspice)
   ½   teaspoon ground ginger
   1   cup cooked and smoothly mashed kabocha
        pumpkin, cooled (or canned pumpkin)
   3   ounces softened cream cheese
   ¾   cup whipping cream (divided use)
   1   tablespoon sour cream
   ½   cup sugar (half white and half brown for added flavor)
   1   teaspoon almond extract

   Cookie crumbs (gingersnaps; amaretti, sugar, or
      spice cookies; or cinnamon-sugar graham crackers)

Tip

Defrost frozen phyllo dough in refrigerator overnight or all day; remove desired number of sheets (and a few extra, in case of accidents). Return phyllo to freezer. To avoid drying and cracking, keep phyllo covered with a lightweight, damp kitchen towel while you work with individual sheets.

Make phyllo cups: Preheat oven to 350 degrees ❖ Stack three sheets of phyllo dough on top of each other and cut into 8 (4-inch) squares ❖ Spray muffin tins with butter-flavored cooking spray ❖ Tuck each stack of squares into a muffin cup ❖ Spray inside of squares lightly with butter-flavored cooking spray ❖ Bake 6 to 7 minutes ❖ Cool on wire rack ❖ Set aside until just before serving.

Make mousse: In a dry frying pan over medium-high heat, toast 5-spice powder, pumpkin pie spice, and ginger, swirling and stirring to prevent scorching, just until aroma is released ❖ Pour into medium bowl ❖ Stir kabocha purée into spices ❖ In a separate bowl, beat softened cream cheese together with 1 to 2 tablespoons whipping cream, to make a smooth, soft mixture ❖ Stir this mixture into the pumpkin purée ❖ With an electric mixer, beat remaining whipping cream until it holds soft peaks; add sour cream and gradually add sugar while continuing to beat; stir in almond extract. Gently fold into pumpkin mixture, using an up–and–over motion, not stirring ❖ Cover and chill until a few minutes before serving time ❖ Just before serving, fill cups, garnishing with a sprinkling of cookie crumbs.

❖ *Serves 8.*

Variations:

To lighten this recipe:
- use low-fat (not nonfat) cream cheese
- use Splenda instead of sugar
- use low-fat or nonfat sour cream and low-fat or nonfat whipping cream
- Garnish with a sliver of fruit instead of cookie crumbs

Figs and cheese

"Make small incisions in as many figs as desired and fill with cream cheese moistened with a little sweet cream and beaten until soft. Serve with crackers and coffee at the end of dinner."

— *Jan. 18, 1929*

In a special cooking section, Louise Kaanapu recalled that, as a small child, she was expected to get up early each morning during mango season. Her job was to collect all the fruit that had fallen in her family's yard during the night. Fruit that was slightly bruised would often be set aside to be roasted whole for the family's dessert. In a time when mango trees graced almost every yard, and every Islander knew the differences between the varieties, Kaanapu was careful to specify the mango types that work best for roasting: MacGuire mangoes were most delicious roasted, she said, but Haden and common Hawaiian types were acceptable. Common Chinese mangoes, she said, were too stringy.

Roasted Mangoes | Appeared Sept. 24, 1989

Whole, peeled mangoes	Cinnamon	Vanilla or *haupia* ice cream
Sugar	Butter	
Nutmeg	Water, if needed	

Preheat oven to 350 degrees ✤ Line a rimmed baking sheet with heavy-duty aluminum foil or nonstick foil ✤ Place whole, peeled mangoes on pan ✤ Top each mango with 1 teaspoon sugar, a light dusting of nutmeg and cinnamon and a couple of small knobs of butter ✤ If the mangoes are just ripe, add a little water to the pan to prevent sticking ✤ Very ripe mangoes will release juice right away ✤ Roast mangoes, uncovered, for 45 minutes to 1 hour ✤ The syrup they release will be served over the cooked fruit ✤ To serve, place a whole mango in each bowl, top with ice cream and drizzle over some of the syrup that formed during cooking ✤ You'll need a full complement of utensils: a knife to cut slices, a fork to eat with, and a spoon to scoop up the delicious juices.

✤ *Serves 1 per mango.*

By 1993, homemade *manju* (Japanese bean-stuffed pastries) had become rare. But food editor Patsy Matsuura found an expert in the art in Sachi Fukuda, a Hilo cookbook author whose *Pupus: An Island Tradition* (Bess Press, 1995) is itself an Island tradition. These confections, meant to be served with tea, may be baked in a Western-style pastry, encased in a cooked rice flour dough, or steamed in a bun. The pastry style is easiest for the home cook—and preferred by the younger generation. These make a nice snack at room temperature, but they'll blow your mind when served hot.

Pie Crust Manju | Appeared March 24, 1993

5	cups flour	Azuki bean paste (recipe follows)
1	teaspoon salt	1 egg yolk
¾	cup water	2 tablespoons evaporated milk
1⅔	cup canola oil	

In a medium bowl, whisk together flour and salt ❖ In a measuring cup, mix together water and oil and drizzle into flour while mixing with fork to blend into a smooth dough ❖ Preheat oven to 400 degrees ❖ Pinch off enough dough to make a 2-inch ball and roll and flatten between the palms of the hands ❖ Place a small ball of azuki bean paste in the center and wrap dough around filling to completely seal ❖ Place sealed-side-down on ungreased cookie sheet ❖ Continue until all the dough has been filled ❖ In a small bowl, whisk together egg yolk and evaporated milk ❖ Lightly brush each *manju* with this glaze ❖ Bake for 20 minutes, or until lightly browned.

❖ *Makes 30 to 40 pastries.*

Azuki Bean Paste

1	(20-ounce) package azuki beans
3¼	cups raw sugar
1	teaspoon salt

Place beans in large bowl, cover with hot water, cover with plastic wrap, and soak for 24 hours, adding more hot water as the beans absorb the liquid ❖ Beans are ready to cook when they can be pierced with a thumbnail ❖ Preheat oven to 450 degrees ❖ Drain beans and place in a 9 x 13–inch baking pan with enough water to barely cover ❖ Cover tightly with foil (beans will not attain the right color and texture if they are not tightly covered during the cooking process) ❖ Bake for 1½ hours, until beans begin to split ❖ When beans are done, drain off any water in excess of ¼ cup ❖ With a potato masher, mash beans and mix in sugar and salt until flavorings are completely dissolved ❖ Cover again with foil, sealing tightly, and continue baking at 450 degrees for another 45 minutes, stirring once, until beans are fairly firm and have absorbed most of the liquid ❖ Remove from oven and cool, covered, for about two hours ❖ Beans are now ready to use, or can be transferred to a zippered plastic bag and frozen.

❖ *Makes 3 cups.*

> ### Azuki bean paste
>
> Azuki bean paste, "an" in Japanese, is sold canned in various forms, most commonly smooth koshi-an or chunky tsubushi-an. If you can't find azuki bean paste, fill the baked *manju* with peanut butter.

Pie crust *manju*, Japanese-style cakes made with a crumbly dough and stuffed with sweet bean paste (or, if you like, peanut butter!), are the perfect foil for a cup of tea and good conversation.

Biko (bee-ko) is one of a family of rice-and-coconut-milk-based sweets that are favored Philippine snacks, sold in small groceries, bake shops, and on the street both in the Philippines and Hawai'i, and often made at home, too. Requiring just a handful of ingredients, biko is very easy to make and dangerously delicious. There's just one tricky point: avoid drowning the rice in the coconut-milk caramel or it will fail to jell. Felicitas Ong Sotelo sent this one in.

✳ Biko: Philippine Sweet Rice "Fudge" | Appeared April 22, 1981

1   pound (a generous 2 cups) white sweet or glutinous rice
2½ cups water
2   cups light brown sugar
2   cups dark brown sugar
2   (13.5-ounce) cans coconut milk

Lightly oil or spray a 9 x 13–inch baking dish ❖ Set aside ❖ Combine rice and water in rice cooker and steam until rice is plump and tender (the rice cooker will turn itself off) ❖ In a saucepan, stir together sugars and coconut milk and bring to a boil ❖ Watch carefully; the mixture can boil over in an instant ❖ Reduce heat to medium and simmer, lightly bubbling, for 15 minutes until caramel is slightly thickened and reduced ❖ Preheat oven to 350 degrees ❖ In the rice cooker pot, combine rice with half the caramel mixture ❖ Spread mixture evenly in oiled baking dish ❖ Slowly and gently spoon most of the remaining caramel over the rice mixture ❖ There should be ⅓-inch or so of coconut-milk caramel floating over the rice and no more; discard any excess caramel ❖ Bake biko until the rice has absorbed the caramel, leaving the shape of the rice visible and no liquid floating on top ❖ Cooking times vary depending on the moisture content of the rice and the amount of caramel used: usually 30 to 45 minutes, but longer baking won't hurt it ❖ If desired, preheat broiler and broil on second shelf (4 to 5 inches from element) for 30 to 60 seconds to further caramelize the surface.

❖ *Serves 15.*

Variations:
- Combine equal parts black or red glutinous rice with white sweet rice. The biko will be a rich eggplant color. To soften the whole grain rice, soak the combined rices in water to cover for 24 hours before baking. Whole grain biko takes much longer to bake, 60 to 90 minutes.
- To make biko without a rice cooker: In a large saucepan, combine 1 pound sweet rice with 5 cups water and bring to a full boil; cover, reduce heat to low, and steam until rice is plump and tender. (If the rice is dry or chewy once all the water has cooked away, add a half cup of boiling water; cover and continue to steam on low.)

Tip

Traditionally, biko is baked in banana leaves (sold in Chinatown, washed and already stripped of the central rib). The leaves must first be softened: turn a burner (electric or gas range) to high and, wearing oven mitts, slowly pass the banana leaf a few inches above the heat. You'll see the leaf change color, turning a shiny bright green and relaxing; it takes just seconds. Press the leaf into the pan, fold and trim to fit.

Sweet rice

Sweet rice (also called glutinous rice or mochi rice) is available in any well-stocked Asian grocery; Milled sweet white rice is most often used for making Japanese pillowy sweets; colored whole-grain sweet rices are favored for Thai, Indonesian, and other cuisines.

Biko, Filipino-style coconut "fudge" made with glutinous ("sticky" or "sweet") rice and a coconut milk caramel, doesn't look like much but disappears as readily as the chocolate variety.

When was the last time you saw a blueberry cream cheese pie? They were everywhere in the '80s and '90s. This lemon-accented, light-textured version was a "My Best Recipe" selection from reader Regina Lo. It's typical of the time in being composed mainly of boxed and canned products. Feel free to substitute 2 cups whipped cream for the Dream Whip (in which case, omit milk but add vanilla to whipped cream). Instead of canned pie filling, fresh blueberries may be cooked with a little sugar. Also, you can use Splenda instead of sugar.

Best Blueberry Cream Cheese Pie | Appeared April 28, 1993

For the crust:
- ¾ cup butter
- ¼ cup brown sugar
- 1¼ cups flour
- ½ cup chopped nuts

For the pie:
- 1 (3-ounce) box lemon-flavored gelatin (Jell-O, if available)
- 1 cup hot water
- 1 (8-ounce) packaged reduced-fat cream cheese (*not* nonfat)
- ½ cup sugar
- ½ teaspoon vanilla extract
- ½ cup milk
- 1 (5.2-ounce) package Dream Whip
- 1 (21-ounce) can blueberry pie filling, chilled

Make the crust: Preheat oven to 375 degrees ✣ Cream together butter and brown sugar ✣ Add flour a little at a time, until well-blended ✣ Add chopped nuts ✣ Pat into a 9 x 13–inch baking pan ✣ Bake for 15 minutes ✣ Cool on rack.

Make the filling: Dissolve Jell-O in hot water and allow to cool ✣ Meanwhile, cream together cream cheese and sugar ✣ Slowly add gelatin, a little at a time, until well-blended ✣ Combine vanilla, milk, and Dream Whip and whip for 5 minutes ✣ Fold into cream cheese mixture, using a gentle up-and-over motion, not stirring ✣ Pour into cooled crust ✣ Chill 1 to 2 hours ✣ Pour blueberry filling over top and chill.

✣ *Serves 12.*

Cookies

"Guests always ask for this recipe," wrote *Advertiser* editors of a light nut-and-date cookie that was included in a story on meringue. But they probably won't ask for the recipe if you try this on a very hot, humid day; meringue-based desserts wilt fast in this kind of weather. To save time, you can use packaged, chopped dates, unavailable when this recipe was published three-quarters of a century ago.

Meringue Cookies | Appeared Aug. 5, 1938

2	egg whites	1	cup chopped, seeded dates
Few grains salt		1	cup chopped walnuts
1	cup sugar	1	teaspoon vanilla extract

Preheat oven to 275 degrees ❖ Place egg whites in bowl and sprinkle with salt; beat with handheld mixer until stiff ❖ Gradually beat in sugar ❖ Place in the top of a double boiler over rapidly boiling water and beat steadily until the mixture appears sugary around the edges ❖ Remove from heat and stir in dates, nuts, and vanilla ❖ Drop small teaspoonfuls onto oil-sprayed or buttered cookie sheet ❖ Bake for 1 hour or until cookies have set; they should be firm and you should be able to remove them from the pan without bending or breaking ❖ Cool on a rack and store in an airtight container.

❖ *Makes 24 cookies.*

Variations:
Serve cookies with ice cream, drizzled with fruit purée or chocolate sauce. Use other soft and sweet dried fruit, such as figs.

"I am of the crisp cookie persuasion," said Kailuan Joan Dowsett Osborne in sharing a recipe for thin, crackling cornflake cookies, a favorite of her family acquired from her friend Marianne Wheeler. Wheeler said the recipe was passed down from her grandmother in Holland, Michigan. The cookies are topped with decorative sugar and Wheeler varies the colors with the season: red and green at Christmas, orange at Halloween, pastels at Easter. (Find the sugar in kitchen supply shops or where baking supplies are sold.)

Cereal Cookies | Appeared Nov. 10, 2004

1 cup butter	3½ cups flour
1 cup vegetable oil	1 teaspoon baking soda
1 cup granulated sugar plus more for decoration	1 teaspoon salt
1 cup brown sugar	1 cup crushed cornflakes
1 teaspoon vanilla extract	1 cup rolled oats
1 egg	½ cup chopped walnuts
1 tablespoon milk	Decorative sugar

Preheat oven to 350 degrees. In a large bowl, cream together butter, oil, granulated sugar, and brown sugar. Add vanilla, egg, and milk and mix until combined. In a second bowl, whisk together flour, baking soda, and salt. Stir dry mixture into wet mixture. Finally, stir in cereals and nuts. Roll lightly between palms to form balls and place on ungreased cookie sheet. Flatten with fork dipped in sugar. Sprinkle with colored sugar. Bake for 12 minutes.

❖ *Makes 5 dozen cookies.*

Twenty years ago, the Garden Café at the Honolulu Academy of Arts was staffed by volunteers who contributed recipes, did the cooking and serving and donated not only the profits but their tips to buy artworks for the gallery. A cadre of 80 women put in one or two mornings a week and this dessert (known in another form as Seven Layer Bars) was among the recipes they shared with reporter Bev Creamer when she wrote about their efforts.

Mardi Gras Bars | Appeared Nov. 30, 1981

½ cup butter	1 cup butterscotch morsels (6 ounces)
1½ cups graham cracker crumbs	1 cup semisweet chocolate morsels
1 cup flaked sweetened coconut	1 (14-ounce) can sweetened condensed milk

Preheat oven to 350 degrees (325 degrees for glass pans) ❖ In a 9 x 13–inch baking pan, melt butter in oven ❖ Remove from oven and sprinkle graham cracker crumbs over butter, followed by layers of coconut, butterscotch morsels, and chocolate morsels ❖ Drizzle condensed milk evenly over all ❖ Bake 25 to 30 minutes, cool and cut into bars.

❖ *Makes 48 small squares (they're very rich).*

Cereal cookies are mother's love on a plate. The secret of success with this crisp throwback is to flatten the cookies well with the tines of a fork.

Soy sauce in a cookie? When you think about it, it's no more weird than sauerkraut in a cake or pepper on strawberries, and all are delicious. This recipe makes use not only of soy sauce but of crunchy miniature Japanese rice crackers called *arare* (ah-rah-RAY). In answer to a query, Myrna C. Ishimoto sent in this recipe, called Shawnie's Favorite, for a friend's nephew who loves these.

❋ Shawnie's Favorite | Appeared March 7, 2007

1½ cups butter	3	cups sifted flour
1 cup brown sugar, packed	1½	teaspoons baking soda
2 teaspoons vanilla extract	1¾	cups puffed rice cereal
1 tablespoon soy sauce		(Rice Krispies, if available)
1 cup milk chocolate chips	1½	cups crushed *kakimochi* (*arare*)

In a large mixing bowl, cream together butter and brown sugar ❖ Stir in vanilla and soy sauce ❖ Add chocolate chips and mix well ❖ Mix in flour and baking soda; blend well ❖ Add cereal and *kakimochi* ❖ Roll into 1-inch balls and place on an ungreased cookie sheet ❖ With a spatula or your hands, flatten balls slightly ❖ Bake until golden brown, about 15 minutes ❖ Remove cookies from cookie sheet and cool on a rack ❖ Store in an airtight container.

❖ *Makes about 6 dozen cookies.*

I was wowed by these cookies when *Advertiser* staffer Shirley Higa brought them to a fundraiser. Almond cookies, made with lard, shortening, or vegetable oil, are a longtime specialty of local Chinese bakeries, but they're often tasteless and overly oily. The perfect almond cookie is crisp and delicately flavored and so irresistible that eating one is impossible. These are pretty much perfect.

> **Tip**
>
> Instead of greasing, and for easier cleanup, line cookie sheets with parchment paper cut to size. First, spray cookie sheets lightly with water or oil spray to keep parchment in place.

Dreamy Almond Delites | From Wanda's Kitchen

1 cup unsalted butter
1 cup sugar
4 cups flour
1 teaspoon baking soda
1 cup vegetable oil (Wesson, if available)
2 teaspoons almond extract

In a large bowl or bowl of a standing mixer, cream butter and sugar until fluffy ❖ Sift flour together with baking soda and combine with butter mixture ❖ Add vegetable oil and almond extract ❖ Cover and refrigerate for 20 minutes ❖ Preheat oven to 325 degrees ❖ Scoop chilled dough out with small ice cream scoop and roll into ball between palms ❖ Place on ungreased baking sheet and flatten slightly ❖ Bake 15 to 18 minutes.

❖ *Makes about 6 dozen 1-inch cookies.*

Subtly sweet, light but crisp, these almond cookies are two-bite bits of heaven, enjoyable for children but sophisticated and subtle enough for an elegant grownup event.

Cakes

Though it's called a bar, this recipe is not a cookie but an airy-light shallow sheet cake, popular on the buffets of various restaurants. If you're assigned dessert for a whole classroom-full or a large party, this will do it. Don't use crushed pineapple; there's too much liquid. The fruit should be dry or the cake will not set: Drain pineapple in colander; press out liquid with paper toweling.

Pineapple Cake Nut Bars | Appeared Dec. 12, 2007

- 3 cups flour
- 1 teaspoon salt
- 1 teaspoon baking soda
- 2 cups roasted macadamia nuts, finely chopped
- 1 cup butter, softened
- 4 cups sugar
- 8 eggs
- 2 (20-ounce) cans pineapple chunks or rings, drained, chopped, and drained again

"Celebrate Pineapple Week with Tempting New Dishes of Hawaii's Luscious Fruit."

— *Dec. 2, 1932*

Preheat oven to 325 degrees ✣ Spray or grease and flour a 12 x 12 –inch jelly roll pan (shallow, rimmed pan) ✣ Set aside ✣ In a medium bowl, whisk together flour, salt, and baking soda; stir in macadamia nuts ✣ Set aside ✣ In a bowl or standing mixer, cream together butter and sugar ✣ Beat in eggs one at a time ✣ Gradually add flour-nut mixture ✣ Stir in pineapple ✣ Spread batter evenly in prepared pans ✣ Place on center rack of preheated oven ✣ Bake until golden brown, edges pull away slightly from pan, center springs back when gently pressed with a finger, and toothpick inserted into the center emerges clean ✣ Cool on rack and cut.

✣ *Makes 40 larger squares or 80 smaller fingers.*

Light and rich, our recipe for Pineapple Macadamia-Nut Cake Bars makes an acre — but take it to a potluck or school event and you won't have any leftovers to bring home.

Honolulu pastry chef Cherilyn Chun, who has worked to perfect her own Dobash Cake recipe, says it's important to use a good-quality cocoa powder. This cake is traditionally served cold. With cupcakes so popular (they encourage portion control and, besides, they're cute), we decided to photograph them in miniature with the aid of Sugar Rush by Frances, a Honolulu catering firm that specializes in miniature desserts.

Chocolate Dobash Cake | Appeared Oct. 30, 1996

For the chocolate chiffon:
- 1¼ cups sugar
- 1½ cups cake flour
- 3 tablespoons unsweetened cocoa powder (i.e. Hershey's Special Dark Cocoa, Ghirardelli, or other dark Dutch-processed, or alkalized, cocoa)
- ½ teaspoon baking soda
- ½ teaspoon salt
- ¾ teaspoon baking powder
- ½ cup oil
- 3 large eggs, beaten
- ½ cup water

For the meringue:
- 8 egg whites
- 1 cup sugar
- Pinch of cream of tartar

For the chocolate Dobash frosting and filling:
- 1½ cups plus ½ cup water
- 1¼ cups sugar
- ½ teaspoon salt
- 2 teaspoons vanilla extract
- 4 tablespoons butter
- ½ cup cocoa
- 3 tablespoons cornstarch

Preheat the oven to 350 degrees ❖ Make the chocolate chiffon: In large bowl, sift together 1¼ cups sugar, cake flour, cocoa, baking soda, salt, and baking powder ❖ In another large bowl, blend together oil, eggs, and water ❖ Using a handheld electric mixer and large bowl, or in bowl of standing mixer, combine dry ingredients with wet and mix on medium 5 minutes.

Make the meringue: In another bowl, scrupulously free of any oil, beat egg whites until triple in volume ❖ Add 1 cup sugar and cream of tartar and continue beating on high until soft peaks form, about 4 minutes ❖ Gently fold meringue into chocolate batter (see "Fear of Meringue") ❖ Measure and pour 3½ cups of batter each into 2 (8-inch) ungreased cake pans ❖ Allow 1 inch of space from the top of the pan. (Do not overfill; make cupcakes with any extra batter.) ❖ Bake at 350 degrees for 30 to 33 minutes or until done ❖ Remove pans from oven and carefully turn pans over onto cooling rack, leaving cakes in the pans to cool ❖ Cool completely. Run knife around outside edge of each pan to loosen cakes ❖ Flip pans over and tap pans to remove cake ❖ Wrap in foil and freeze until firm.

Island bakeries took a Hungarian classic and made it their own, reinterpreting a layered torte as a chiffon cake, topped with three different frostings — chocolate pudding glaze, chantilly cream and "dream" icing (whipped cream with chocolate sprinkles).

Make chocolate Dobash filling and frosting: In a saucepan, combine water, sugar, salt, vanilla, butter, and cocoa into saucepan ✤ Stir; bring to a boil over medium to low heat, being careful not to allow mixture to scorch or burn ✤ Remove from heat, momentarily ✤ Whisk together ½ cup water and cornstarch ✤ Add to cocoa mixture, whisking continuously ✤ Return to stove and cook until mixture is thick and translucent ✤ Pour into clean bowl, cool, cover, and refrigerate ✤ Use as filling between layers of cake and to ice cake ✤ Garnish with a maraschino cherry, if desired.

✤ *Serves 8.*

Variations:

• **Crumb topping:**
  Make crumbs with baked extra batter and sprinkle on top or press around sides of iced cake.

• **Chantilly cream:**
  Fill and ice cake with Chantilly cream. In a saucepan, combine 1 tablespoon vanilla, 1½ pounds butter (6 sticks), 2 cups evaporated milk, 8 ounces margarine (2 sticks), 2 whole eggs, and 1 egg yolk. Place over medium heat and whisk to combine. Add 2½ cups sugar, stirring constantly, and bring to a low boil. Whisk in 1½ tablespoons arrowroot or cornstarch. Turn off heat and allow mixture to stand for 15 minutes. Pour into clean bowl, cool, and refrigerate. Soften slightly at room temperature before frosting.

• **Dream Cake:**
  Frost Dobosh Cake with whipped cream and sprinkle with dark chocolate curls. To make stable whipped cream, combine 1 pint whipped cream with 2 tablespoons sugar and 2 tablespoons sour cream. Keep frosted cake chilled.

What's Dobash, anyway?

The confection Islanders know and love as Dobash cake couldn't be farther from the original.

The Dobos torte was invented by a Hungarian baker so famous there's a museum of gastronomy in Budapest that bears his name. He was a chef, pâtissier, importer, and culinary promoter named József C. Dobos (1847-1924). His cake, first introduced in 1887, was composed of multiple layers (5 or 7) of genoise (a sponge cake) with buttercream filling and a caramel glaze topping.

The cake that became known as "Dobash" is said to have been brought to Hawai'i by someone from Robert's Bakery in Hilo in the 1960s, who had enjoyed the sweet during a trip to Europe. (Dobos torte is practically the national cake of Hungary.) In the Islands, the cake morphed into chocolate chiffon with chocolate pudding or Chantilly cream icing, often coated with cake crumbs.

Fear of Meringue: The Cure

The primary leavener in chiffon cakes, such as the Dobash cake on this page, is meringue — beaten egg whites.
- Beaters and bowl must be squeaky clean, free of grease or oil
- Whites must be absolutely free of any yolk
- Separate whites one at a time into a small bowl; if yolk is accidentally pierced, only one egg will be affected
- To separate eggs, break with one hand and pour into the other, allowing white to run through slightly splayed fingers, keeping yolk in hand
- For maximum volume, whites should be at room temperature; to hasten process, place whites in bowl and place bowl in warm water
- To fold meringue into batter without deflating it, use 2-inch wide spatula and an up-and-over motion; do not stir in circles. Place one third of meringue on top of batter; scoop batter from bottom of bowl and gently bring batter up and over meringue, incorporating the two with as few strokes as possible. Add remaining two-thirds of meringue and continue.
- Do not over-incorporate; a few slight streaks of white meringue in the batter are fine.
- Use "mistakes" for scrambled eggs or omelets; leftover yolks for custard pie or crème brûlée.

Among the sweetest memories of my childhood is visiting my godmother, Cyrilla Medeiros of Wailuku, where there were always cookies and where, on some memorable occasions, there was this amazing chocolate cake with a creamy filling and a cloud-white, cloud-light frosting. Whenever she would make this cake for dessert, the next day her two sons would vie to beat each other home from school to be first at the leftovers. The technique here is modernized but the cake is still almost brownie-like — crisp without, tender within.

Black Magic Cake | Appeared May 2, 2008

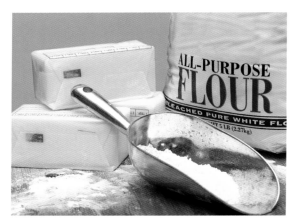

4	tablespoons vegetable shortening (Crisco, if available)
4	squares Baker's unsweetened chocolate (see Note)
1	teaspoon plus ½ teaspoon vanilla extract
2	cups sugar
½	teaspoon salt
2	egg yolks
1	cup room temperature milk
2	cups sifted cake flour
1	teaspoon baking soda
1	teaspoon baking powder

Preheat oven to 350 degrees ❖ Line 2 (8-inch) metal cake pans with parchment or waxed paper; grease or spray with oil-flour spray ❖ Set aside ❖ Place Crisco and chocolate in a microwave oven–proof bowl; microwave on Medium for 1 minute, stir, then continue to microwave, stopping at 30-second intervals to stir, until chocolate is melted and Crisco is incorporated ❖ Add 1 teaspoon vanilla extract and set aside to cool to room temperature ❖ In a bowl, mix together sugar and salt ❖ In another bowl, beat together yolks, milk, and ½ teaspoon vanilla ❖ Into another bowl, sift together cake flour, baking soda, and baking powder ❖ With an electric mixer, or in the bowl of a standing mixer, blend and mix chocolate mixture and sugar-salt mixture ❖ In 3 batches, alternately add flour mixture and egg mixture ❖ Work quickly and do not overmix ❖ Divide batter equally between prepared pans ❖ Bake on middle rack for 28 to 30 minutes ❖ Sides of the cake will separate very slightly from the pans ❖ Cool on a rack, fill with Mrs. Pombo's Vanilla Filling (recipe follows) and frost with 7-Minute Icing (recipe follows).

❖ *Serves 8 to 10.*

"Add a dash of ground ginger to chocolate frosting."
— *April 14, 1949*

Note: Instead of Baker's unsweetened chocolate, use an even higher quality of unsweetened chocolate, such as Scharffen Berger, if desired.

Variation:
Add ¼ cup Valhrona or other dark cocoa and 1 teaspoon instant coffee powder for even deeper chocolate flavor.

This is my godmother's mother's recipe for old-fashioned cooked cake filling. You need a double boiler; if you don't own one, use a metal or other heatproof bowl perched atop a saucepan. It's very important that the bottom of the top pan not touch the water below and that the water be gently simmering, not boiling.

Mrs. Pombo's Vanilla Filling

3	tablespoons cornstarch	1	egg
1/3	cup sugar	1	cup milk
1/8	teaspoon salt	1	teaspoon vanilla extract, or more, to taste

Heat water in bottom of double boiler just to simmering ❖ In the top pan, off the heat, whisk together the cornstarch, sugar, and salt ❖ In a small bowl or measuring cup, beat together the egg and milk ❖ Gradually add these to the cornstarch mixture, whisking constantly to prevent lumps ❖ Place the top pan over the simmering water and whisk constantly until the mixture thickens, scraping the bottom and keeping the mixture moving at all times ❖ This takes a few minutes, but when the thickening happens, it will be very rapid, and this is when lumps can form ❖ When thickened, remove mixture from heat and whisk in vanilla. Allow to cool.

❖ *Fills 1 (8-inch) cake.*

This cooked whipped icing was a common choice in the days when people made cakes from scratch, and it's actually a snap. The hardest part is holding the mixer for 7 minutes or more. Again, you need a double boiler.

7-Minute Icing

2	egg whites (not a trace of yolk)	3	tablespoons water
1	cup sugar	1/2	teaspoon cream of tartar

Bring water to a simmer in the bottom of a double boiler ❖ Meanwhile, off the heat, combine all ingredients and whisk to combine ❖ Place over heat and use a handheld mixer to beat the mixture for 7 to 12 minutes, moving in a circular motion to prevent overcooking at the bottom of the mixture and occasionally scraping with a heat-proof spatula ❖ Again, it's important that the bottom of the pan not touch the water and that the water be gently simmering, not boiling ❖ Beat until mixture has tripled in volume, is glossy, and holds peaks ❖ Recipe may be doubled if you're making a larger cake or like a lot of frosting.

❖ *Frosts 1 (8-inch) cake.*

Variation:
When the icing is done, add well-drained fruit, such as prunes if you're making a prune or spice cake; or a few drops of food coloring, if desired.

In 1931, Mrs. Augustus E. Murphy won a cooking competition with this multilayered confection — a creamy cottage cheesecake atop a crust that's somewhere between a cake and a cookie. She received "one of Miss Jessie Marie DeBoth's famous cook books," but in her photograph, she doesn't look any too happy about it. We've modernized this a bit.

Mrs. Murphy's Cottage Cheesecake | Appeared March 13, 1931

1	pound cottage cheese	1	cup sugar
2	tablespoons cornstarch		Zest and juice of 1 lemon
1	cup cream	3	egg whites, beaten to soft peaks
2	tablespoons melted butter		Cake Crust (recipe follows)
3	egg yolks		

Place cottage cheese in fine-mesh sieve and allow to drain, stirring occasionally and pressing lightly with the back of a large spoon ❖ Preheat oven to 325 degrees ❖ Place cornstarch in a small bowl and whisk to reduce lumps; drizzle in a little of the cream to make a slurry, whisking constantly ❖ Whisk in remaining cream and set aside ❖ In the bowl of a food processor, process cottage cheese, melted butter, egg yolks, sugar, cornstarch-cream mixture and lemon ❖ Scrape into a large bowl ❖ Gently fold in the egg whites with an up an over motion, not stirring ❖ Place crust dough (see below) in an 8-by-8-inch baking dish and pat down with fingers ❖ Pour cheese mixture over crust and bake in center of oven at 325 degrees for 60 to 75 minutes ❖ Top will be a darkish brown; skewer in center emerges clean.

❖ *Makes 10 to 12, depending on size of bars or squares.*

Cake Crust:

1	cup flour
1/2	teaspoon baking powder
1/4	cup sugar
1/8	teaspoon salt
2	tablespoons cold butter
1	egg
1	teaspoon vanilla extract

In a bowl, whisk together flour, baking powder, sugar, and salt ❖ Rub in cold butter with your fingers (rub butter and flour between thumb and fingers, or rub onto the sides of the bowl, until incorporated) ❖ In a small bowl, whisk together egg and vanilla ❖ Stir into flour mixture; dough will be rather dry and crumbly.

Idea

Give leftover fruitcake or other dense cakes a second life: Cut into chunks, spread softened ice cream in a flat baking dish, sprinkle chunks over, then gently combine. Place in dessert dishes or wine glasses and pour over a few drops of liqueur, brandy, or rum.
— *Appeared Feb. 17, 1982*

Senator Norman Mizuguchi wooed voters with free recipe booklets that have become collector's items. This cake recipe spread throughout the Islands from a "best of" collection he issued in the 1980s.

Norman Mizuguchi's Chocolate Chip Date Cake | Appeared Oct. 13, 1982

8 ounces dried dates, pitted and chopped
1½ teaspoons plus 1¼ teaspoon baking soda
2½ cups boiling water
¾ cup butter, softened
1½ cups sugar
3 eggs
2¼ cups flour
¾ teaspoon salt
½ cup chopped walnuts
1 (6-ounce) package semisweet chocolate chips
Sugar

Preheat oven to 350 degrees ✴ Grease or spray a 9 x 13–inch baking dish ✴ In a bowl, combine dates and 1½ teaspoons baking soda and pour boiling water over them ✴ Mix well; set aside to cool ✴ In a large bowl, cream together butter and sugar until light and fluffy ✴ Thoroughly beat in eggs ✴ In a medium bowl, sift together flour, salt, and remaining baking soda ✴ Alternately stir date mixture and flour mixture into creamed butter mixture, ending with dry ingredients and mixing thoroughly between additions ✴ Pour into prepared baking dish ✴ Sprinkle walnuts, chocolate pieces, and a little sugar over top ✴ Bake for 40 to 50 minutes or until skewer emerges clean.

✴ Serves 15 to 18.

Former State Senate President Norman Mizuguchi takes credit for being the first legislator to use food to attract votes by means of free recipe booklets. Those booklets, which began with "Favorite Recipes of Norman Mizuguchi" in 1976, and continues with several subsequent publications during Mizuguchi's long tenure, are now collector's items, and many of his recipes are found, uncredited, in community cookbooks here. Throughout the '70s and '80s, other legislators published booklets, or passed out index cards printed with favorite recipes, or added recipes to their political mailings. Another way that politicos have contributed to Island foodways is the stew-rice fundraiser; $1.50 for a heaping plate and a speech.

"Candy season is here again."
— Nov. 8, 1935

Candy

In 1989, Sabrina Vierra, a Kaçu High School home economics student, turned nuts into cash, winning the $5,000 grand prize in a Baker's Chocolate Recipe Contest with her Hawaiian Turtles candy. She formed the candies into the traditional turtle shape, painstakingly laying out nuts; I found it much easier to roughly chop the nuts and mix them into the caramel. You need to grate a little paraffin (edible wax) into both the caramel and the chocolate so they will harden. Caramels can be hard to find; Brach's makes them, as does Goetze's (Caramel Creams). Those old-fashioned Kraft squares are available via mail-order from www.oldtimecandy.com.

Hawaiian Turtles | Appeared Nov. 8, 1989

- 16 ounces caramels (about 60)
- 3 tablespoons water
- ¼ cup plus ¼ cup shaved paraffin wax
- 12 ounces dry-roasted macadamia nuts, roughly chopped
- 8 ounces good-quality bittersweet or semisweet chocolate

Place caramels and water in a microwave-safe bowl ✦ Microwave on Medium for 1 minute; stir and add ¼ cup paraffin wax shaved with a vegetable peeler ✦ Return to microwave and microwave on Medium for another 30 seconds, stopping to stir and continuing at 30-second intervals, until caramels are melted ✦ Stir in macadamia nuts and set aside to cool. In another microwave-safe bowl, break up chocolate and microwave on Medium for 1 minute; stir and add ¼ cup wax; continue microwaving on Medium, stopping at 30-second intervals to stir until melted ✦ Set aside to cool to lukewarm ✦ Spoon rounded teaspoonfuls of warm caramel nut mixture onto a baking sheet lined with waxed paper or parchment paper, forming round, lumpy patties ✦ If the caramel remains soft after a few minutes, place tray in freezer briefly ✦ Spoon about 1 teaspoon of melted chocolate, cooled to lukewarm, atop the caramel patties ✦ Garnish with coconut ✦ Refrigerate, uncovered, until fully set ✦ Store in airtight container in refrigerator.

✦ *Makes about 24 candies.*

Honolulu's Chinese bakeries have been disappearing at a dismaying rate and many of their specialties are simply impossible to reproduce in a home setting. But this candy is one that the home cook can handle; the longer you boil it, the harder the candy will be.

Sesame Peanut Candy | Appeared April 3, 2008

- 2 pounds brown sugar
- ¼ cup vinegar
- ¼ cup water
- 2 pounds roasted, shelled peanuts
- ½ cup sesame seeds, toasted

In a saucepan, dissolve sugar in vinegar and water and boil until quite thick, stirring from time to time to prevent scorching. (The thicker and longer-cooked the sugar solution, the more brittle the candy.) ✦ Pour peanuts into saucepan and mix well ✦ Sprinkle the bottom of a low-rimmed pan or a smooth, clean cutting board with ¾ of the toasted sesame seeds ✦ Pour the peanut mixture into the pan or on the board, flattening it out by rolling over it with a bottle or tall glass smeared with enough peanut oil to keep the candy from sticking to it ✦ Once the top is smooth, even, and flat, sprinkle with remaining sesame seeds ✦ Allow to cool; cut into squares or diamonds.

CHAPTER 6

On the Menu

RESTAURANT RECIPES
OVER THE YEARS

Many of these restaurants and their chefs or owners may be gone, but their food lingers in our memories. The majority of the recipe requests I get at the *Advertiser* are for long-gone restaurant recipes, many of them difficult or impossible to find or reproduce in a home kitchen. But all of these are dishes that worked well when I tested them. Bon appétit!

Restaurateur Michel Martin, who came to the Islands from his native Nice just after World War I and died here at age 100 in 2008, is credited with introducing Islanders to straightforward bistro-style French cooking in a tiny, one-man cafe he opened in out-of-the-way Waipahu during World War II. In the 1960s, he oversaw two eponymous restaurants in Honolulu, where more elaborate classics were the fare. But, always, his mother's French onion soup was on the menu. In 2003, when he was 95 and still an active partner in a small patisserie in Kahala, he told me that the reasons for the soup on that first menu were prosaic: onions are cheap and the soup can be made ahead of time.

Michel's French Onion Soup | Appeared Feb. 26, 2003

4 large onions	Salt and freshly ground pepper
4 tablespoons butter	Freshly grated Parmesan cheese, about 1 cup
2 cloves garlic, thinly sliced	Day-old French bread
$\frac{1}{2}$ cup white wine or dry sherry	(8 baguette slices or 4 larger slices)
4 (10.5-ounce) cans consommé or rich homemade beef broth (about 5$\frac{1}{2}$ cups)	

Peel and thinly slice onions and cut into fourths ✤ In a large, heavy-bottomed soup pot or Dutch oven, over medium heat, gently melt butter; add onions and garlic and cook over low heat slowly, stirring occasionally, until they achieve an even light golden brown ✤ Add wine or sherry and cook until liquid is mostly absorbed ✤ Add consommé or beef stock and bring to a boiling point; reduce heat and simmer 10 to 20 minutes ✤ Add salt and pepper to taste ✤ Refrigerate overnight to allow flavors to develop ✤ Before serving, add $\frac{1}{2}$ cup of Parmesan cheese to the soup and heat soup to serving temperature ✤ Preheat broiler ✤ Place four heatproof soup dishes on a baking sheet and spoon soup into each ✤ Arrange 1 or 2 bread slices on top of each serving and scatter remaining cheese over bread and soup ✤ Place soup bowls on second rack (4 to 5 inches from broiler) and broil 1 minute, or until golden.

✤ *Serves 4 generously.*

From one of the Islands' best-known and most-missed restaurateurs comes a dish that is both sophisticated and simple: Michel's French Onion Soup, on the menu of every restaurant the late Michel Martin ever owned.

George "Cass" Castagnola's Sicilian-style kitchens were great favorites with O'ahu diners in the '70s, '80s, and '90s, and they live on in a cluster of restaurants operated by his former line cooks (most of them of Chinese or Vietnamese descent). Though my personal favorite is his Sicilian chicken with roasted potatoes, it was hard to say no to his decadent and oh-so-garlicky scampi, a great dish when you're trying to impress company. Use the best quality shrimp you can find, although if you opt for frozen, it won't be a tragedy. We've altered the order of the tasks in this recipe to fit the needs of the home cook, and added some fresh basil, but otherwise, the recipe is Castagnola's.

Castagnola's Shrimp Scampi | Appeared Oct. 2, 1991

2 pounds raw jumbo shrimp (shelled and deveined, tail on)
1 teaspoon salt
1 pound linguine pasta
8 large cloves garlic, peeled
4 tablespoons extra-virgin olive oil plus a little more for drizzling over pasta
1 tablespoon dry basil
Fresh ground black pepper to taste
4 ounces (1/2 cup) dry white wine
8 tablespoons butter
4 tablespoons minced Italian (flat-leaf) parsley, plus more for garnish
4 tablespoons thinly sliced (chiffonade) fresh basil

Preheat oven to its lowest temperature and place a heatproof bowl and a serving platter inside ✤ While cleaning shrimp, bring 3 quarts of water to a boil ✤ Add 1 teaspoon salt to boiling water ✤ Boil pasta until just al dente; drain, toss with a drizzle of olive oil to prevent sticking and place on platter in oven to remain warm ✤ Turn off oven ✤ Meanwhile, while keeping an eye on the pasta, make garlic oil: In a large cast-iron skillet (or other heavy-bottomed frying pan), sauté 4 whole cloves of garlic on low heat until just golden; do not burn or scorch ✤ Chop remaining garlic and set aside ✤ Remove caramelized garlic from oil; discard oil or reserve for another use.

Prepare shrimp: Raise temperature of garlic oil to medium, add shrimp, salt, dry basil and pepper ✤ Sauté until shrimp turn pink ✤ Remove shrimp and place in warmed bowl (do not return to oven) ✤ Add reserved chopped garlic to skillet and simmer over medium heat just until golden about 1 minute (do not allow to brown and burn) ✤ Add wine, cut in butter, stir until butter is just relaxed but not fully melted ✤ Sauce should have a creamy texture ✤ Place shrimp in sauce, then arrange over pasta ✤ Sprinkle fresh basil and parsley over shrimp and pasta ✤ Serve immediately.

✤ *Serves 4.*

Restaurateur "Cass" Castagnola's scampi pleases garlic-loving guests as much today as it did when he introduced it to Hawai'i decades ago.

The Swiss Inn occupied an unlikely location — a storefront in a small shopping mall a few miles out of Honolulu. But chef Martin Wyss' mastery of what was then known as "continental" cuisine was such that the restaurant was a favorite of Oahuans for years. Wyss' classic Roesti Potatoes were often served with dishes such as Veal Emince — thin-sliced cutlets in a mushroom cream sauce — the crisp texture of the potatoes contrasting with the richness of the sauce.

Martin Wyss' Roesti Potatoes | Appeared May 25, 1983

¼ cup butter	½ slice bacon, chopped fine
1 teaspoon finely minced onion	1 cup grated cooked potatoes (see Note)

In a small (8-inch or so) crêpe, sauté, or frying pan, melt butter ✤ Add onion and bacon and sauté a few minutes, until onion is limp and translucent and bacon begins to crisp ✤ Add hash browns, mix with fork and press with spatula to form a round cake ✤ Cook over medium heat until golden brown ✤ Run a flexible spatula around the edge and slightly under, then, using two flexible spatulas, carefully flip potato cake and brown on bottom until crisp and golden.

✤ *Serves 2.*

Note: Use all-purpose or boiling potatoes, peeled and simmered until slightly undercooked (may be pierced with a fork, but neither soft nor crumbling), then grate.

The Crouching Lion restaurant, named for the shape of the rugged ridge that overlooked it, was long a favorite stop on the long drive from the Windward side to the North Shore of O'ahu. The restaurant closed in 2007, but in its heyday, it was famous for a Slavonic steak, the delight of garlic-lovers. Slavonic means in the style of the Slavs — but why the steak should be called that isn't clear. What is clear is that it's easy to prepare. Make sure the grill is very hot; a wood-burning grill is best, charcoal is acceptable, gas lends the least smoky flavor. The restaurant once made these steaks tableside, on individual hibachi grills.

Slavonic Steak | Appeared Oct. 1, 1970

1 (7-ounce) tenderloin steak	½ cup vegetable oil
1 tablespoon cracked pepper	5 tablespoons butter
Dash of Italian seasoning	3 cloves garlic, minced

Place steak in flat dish and rub all over with pepper and Italian seasoning ✤ Pour oil into dish; cover with plastic wrap and refrigerate overnight ✤ The next day, bring to room temperature while you heat a grill ✤ Grill (or broil) to desired doneness ✤ Meanwhile, in a small saucepan, melt the butter over medium heat; add minced garlic and cook just until the garlic is golden and fragrant ✤ Remove steak from grill to cutting board; allow to rest a few minutes, then cut into strips and serve on warm plate, dressed with garlic butter.

✤ *Serves 1 as an entrée, 2 to 3 as appetizer.*

This recipe, from Kris Vilassakanod of the now-gone but much-missed Siam Orchid Thai Restaurant, makes use of Thai curry paste, a great ingredient to have in your refrigerator as it lasts almost forever and will lift any Southeast Asian dish to new heights of heat and flavor layers. The paste combines chiles, onion, garlic, galangal (a ginger-like root), lemongrass, kaffir lime leaves, salt, and spices. Panaeng is a drier curry paste, made with less coconut milk than many other curry types and without vegetables. Note that the curry paste is first fried, to release the flavorful oils in the ingredients.

✿ Thai Panaeng Chicken Curry | Appeared Aug. 1, 1990

- ⅓ cup vegetable oil
- 1 tablespoon Thai panaeng curry paste
- ½ pound boneless chicken slices (thigh or breast)
- 7 ounces coconut milk (half a can)
- 2 tablespoons nam pla (fish sauce)
- 1 tablespoon sugar
- Chili or chili-garlic sauce (optional, as desired)
- 12 leaves Thai basil (not Italian basil)
- 1 tablespoon finely sliced kaffir lime leaves
- 2 tablespoons ground dry-roasted peanuts
- Hot Thai-style sticky rice (sweet rice or glutinous rice)

In a heavy-bottomed pan or wok, heat vegetable oil and stir in curry paste; cook until aroma is released ✣ Add chicken pieces and cook, stirring from time to time, until chicken changes color ✣ Add coconut milk, fish sauce, and sugar, and cook until thickened ✣ Add chili or chili-garlic sauce, if more heat is desired ✣ Add basil, kaffir lime leaves, and ground nuts ✣ Stir ✣ Serve with hot sticky rice.

✣ *Serves 4.*

"Add a few drops of
  vinegar or lemon juice to rice
  in cooking; keeps it white and keeps
  grains whole and also allows the rice
  to keep longer on the counter."

— *Sept. 30, 1960*

Here's one way chef Wayne Hirabayashi of the Kahala Hotel & Resort likes to prepare farm-raised Kona Kampachi (called *kāhala* when it's caught wild). You can use any fragrant, moist, white-fleshed fish). He uses kabayaki sauce (so-called eel sauce, a commercial product; substitute teriyaki sauce or equal parts shoyu and mirin and ½ part sugar).

Kampachi Kahala-Style | Appeared April 16, 2008

4   (6-ounce) fillets Kona Kampachi, skin-on, bones removed
Sea salt and freshly ground pepper
2   ounces grape seed oil
4-5 ounces kabayaki sauce (eel-based sauce; if unavailable, use soy sauce)
1   ounce white truffle oil (optional)
1   tablespoon toasted sesame seeds
1   tablespoon grated fresh ginger
12 ounces braised Swiss chard or other greens
12 ounces mushrooms, thinly sliced
1   tablespoon finely cut green onions

Preheat oven to 350 degrees ❖ Season fish with salt and pepper as desired ❖ Heat grape seed oil until hot and add the seasoned fillets, skin-side down; allowing skin to crisp; turn after 4 to 5 minutes ❖ Meanwhile, combine kabayaki sauce and truffle oil; place in a small saucepan and keep warm ❖ Place fish in a baking dish or ovenproof pan, cover with ginger and sesame seeds and bake for 2 to 3 minutes ❖ Meanwhile, in a sauté pan or wok, quickly sauté chard, mushrooms, and green onions together until chard is wilted and mushrooms are softened; season with salt and pepper ❖ To serve: Place mushroom-chard mixture on plate, place fish on top ❖ Drizzle eel sauce over and around ❖ Garnish with deep-fried lotus root, if desired.

❖ *Serves 4.*

How to fillet a whole fish

- Ask the shop to gut and scale the fish
- Use a thin- and narrow-bladed, flexible and very sharp knife
- Remove the head, cutting the collar in a V-shape around the gills
- Remove tail, unless you're serving the fish whole or butterflied
- On a large cutting board, hold the fish firmly in place with one hand, and run the knife from head to tail along one side of the backbone
- Cut along the backbone and open the fish to butterfly it (if you are planning to stuff it or barbecue it, for example) or cut all the way through to split fish in half
- There's a bone in the center of most fish; run a finger along it and feel for the tiny bones. Pull out with needle-nose pliers.
- For fillets, remove backbone and cut halves crosswise into the desired size of fillet.

— *Hints from Kahala Hotel & Resort executive chef Wayne Hirabayashi*

The Yum Yum Tree was a family restaurant chain known for its pies. This sinfully rich pie, in particular, lives on in Islanders' memories even though the restaurants have closed. Several readers requested it. Safety note: this dish contains raw eggs; use pasteurized eggs, if available.

English Toffee Pie | Appeared May 24, 2006

For the crust:

- 1/4 cup butter, softened
- 1/3 cup flour
- 1 1/4 cups brown sugar, packed
- 1/3 cup semisweet chocolate chips
- 1/4 teaspoon salt
- 1/3 cup chopped walnuts
- 1/2 teaspoon vanilla extract
- 1 tablespoon cold water

For the filling:

- 1 1/3 cup butter or margarine, softened
- 1 1/3 cups sugar
- 2 1/2 tablespoons bitter chocolate, chopped
- 3 egg yolks, chilled
- 1 1/4 teaspoons instant chocolate granules (e.g. Nestlé's Quik)

Preheat oven to 350 degrees ✤ Make the crust: Cut butter into flour using pastry cutter or two forks or knives ✤ Add sugar, chocolate chips, and salt, and mix ✤ Add walnuts, vanilla, and cold water ✤ Mix ✤ Press into a lightly floured 9-inch pie pan ✤ Bake for 10 minutes ✤ Cool.

Make the filling: Cream together butter and sugar ✤ Melt chocolate, add to creamed mixture ✤ Stir in one egg yolk; mix until smooth ✤ Add remaining yolks and instant granules; blend ✤ Pour into baked pie shell ✤ Refrigerate overnight ✤ Decorate with whipped cream and chocolate curls.

✤ *Serves 8.*

For many years, Maple Garden was regarded as one of the best Chinese restaurants in the city and owner-manager Robert Hsu one of Honolulu's most gracious hosts, ever willing to explain menu items to those less familiar with Chinese foods. Hsu died in 2008 but is remembered for his version of spicy eggplant with pork, which came as a revelation to many familiar only with relatively tame Cantonese-style dishes.

Eggplant with Hot Garlic Sauce | Appeared April 24, 1991

- 1 teaspoon minced ginger
- 1 teaspoon minced garlic
- 1½ tablespoons soy sauce
- 1 teaspoon sugar
- 1 teaspoon white vinegar
- 1 teaspoon minced fresh red chile pepper or ¼ teaspoon dried red pepper flakes
- 1 teaspoon cornstarch
- 1 cup vegetable oil for frying
- ½-¾ of a round eggplant, peeled and cut into inch-long strips
- ½ cup boneless pork, sliced into strips

To make sauce: in a small bowl, mix together ginger, garlic, soy sauce, sugar, vinegar, chile pepper and cornstarch ❖ Whisk together and set aside ❖ Heat oil in large, heavy frying pan or wok until very hot ❖ Add eggplant ❖ Fry until the pulp is browned but not burned ❖ Place eggplant between paper towels and lightly press to extract excess oil ❖ Add pork to pan and fry about 1 minute until pork is cooked through ❖ Remove pork and discard oil ❖ Heat sauce in same pan until boiling; stir in eggplant and pork ❖ Cook, stirring, until thoroughly heated ❖ Serve hot with hot rice.

❖ *Serves 2.*

Variation:
To reduce oil, microwave eggplant instead of frying it: cut eggplant in half lengthwise. Spray with water and microwave on High for 3 minutes, or longer until tender.

Hale Vietnam restaurant in Kaimukī was among the earliest to introduce Vietnamese food to Oʻahu diners. Serve Dry Noodles as a salad side dish or light lunch; add slivers of barbecued beef or fried tofu for a little more heft. Rice sticks are thin round noodles made from rice flour; vermicelli is an okay-but-not-the-same substitute. Sweet and nearly seedless, Japanese or English cucumbers are preferred here.

 Vietnamese Dry Noodle Salad with Fish Sauce Drizzle | Appeared April 24, 1991

- ¼ pound rice sticks (banh pho), immersed in 1 cup water until soft and translucent
- ½ cup bean sprouts
- ½ bunch fresh mint, washed, leaves only; chopped just before use
- ½ cup cucumber, unpeeled and coarsely chopped
- 4 tablespoons crushed dry-roasted peanuts
- Cilantro leaves
- Fish Sauce Drizzle (recipe follows)

Boil a pot of water and cook noodles until soft, then place under cold running water to stop cooking ❖ Drain ❖ Using scissors, cut into smaller pieces ❖ In a bowl, place the bean sprouts at the bottom, add the rice noodles and top with remaining vegetables ❖ Add barbecued meats or fried tofu, if desired ❖ Sprinkle with crushed peanuts and sprigs of cilantro ❖ Top with Fish Sauce Drizzle to taste.

❖ *Serves 2.*

Fish Sauce Drizzle

- 1 clove garlic
- ½ fresh, hot chile pepper or 2 dried chiles
- Juice and pulp of ½ fresh lime
- 2 tablespoons nam pla (fish sauce)
- 2½ tablespoons water

Peel 1 clove garlic ❖ Split chile pepper or 2 dried chiles, remove seeds and membrane ❖ Cut into pieces and place in a Thai-style stone mortar and pound into a paste with pestle (or use a mini food processor) ❖ Squeeze the lime juice over the paste; dig out lime pulp with small knife and add to paste, mashing well ❖ Add 2 tablespoons fish sauce and water (more if necessary to make a thin drizzle) ❖ Drizzle over rice noodle salad.

❖ *Makes ¾ cup.*

Beau Soleil was a lovely, sun-washed Mediterranean restaurant and deli in Kaimukī operated by caterers Mouman and Holly El-Hajji. A reader requested their recipe for potato salad, spiked with capers, a welcome break from the usual potato-mac.

Beau Soleil Aegean Potato Salad | Appeared Feb. 7, 1996

3	pounds red potatoes, quartered		1	medium sweet onion, thinly sliced
4	tablespoons extra-virgin olive oil		1/2	tablespoon torn fresh mint leaves
3	tablespoons red wine vinegar		1/2	tablespoon minced Italian (flat-leaf) parsley
1/3	cup crumbled feta cheese			Salt and pepper to taste
1/4	cup rinsed and drained capers			

Cook potatoes in salted water until fork-tender ❖ Drain and rinse immediately in cold water to stop cooking ❖ While still warm, add remaining ingredients and toss ❖ Serve warm or cold.

❖ *Serves 6 to 8.*

Chai Chaowasaree is an extremely gracious host, appreciated both for the traditional restaurant, Singha Thai, that he operates in Waikīkī with his sister, and for the contemporary East-West cuisine at Chai's Island Bistro at Aloha Tower Marketplace. Some years ago, he not only honored a reader's request for Singha's Pineapple and Shrimp Fried Rice, he brought some by the office so we could sample it. This recipe may be doubled or tripled so long as you have a big enough wok and high enough heat.

Singha's Pineapple and Shrimp Fried Rice | Appeared April 24, 1996

2	tablespoons vegetable oil		1	tablespoon soy sauce
6	ounces raw shrimp, peeled and deveined		1/2	teaspoon ketchup
1	clove garlic, chopped		1/3	teaspoon sugar
1	egg			Black or white pepper to taste
3	ounces drained pineapple chunks		1	cup steamed long-grain rice, cooked and cooled (can be made with leftovers from the night before)
1	tablespoon thinly sliced onion, broken into crescents			

Heat oil in a large wok or skillet ❖ When the pan is hot, add shrimp and garlic and stir-fry 1 minute or until garlic turns light brown ❖ Add egg and scramble quickly in the pan; add remaining ingredients and stir-fry, tossing or stirring, for a few minutes or until shrimp is thoroughly cooked.

❖ *Serves 2.*

McCully Chop Sui, at the corner of South King and McCully Streets, was a favorite of late-working restaurant workers for its late hours at a time when it was difficult to find anything to eat in Honolulu after 9 p.m. People loved the sizzling platters (sometimes so many were ordered at once the smoke would hang in the air) and this Singapore-style chow fun (fun or fan is Cantonese for noodle; in this case, look fun—wide, flat, silky-textured rice noodles—is used).

 Singapore Chow Fun | Appeared Sept. 12, 1984

- ½   pound wide, flat rice noodles
  (look fun or chow fun, fresh or dried)
- 2   teaspoons vegetable oil for frying
- 1   clove garlic, smashed
- 1   egg
- ¼   cup celery, thinly sliced at an angle
- ¼   cup chopped onion, sliced and broken
  into crescents
- 1   cup bean sprouts
- 1   cooked Chinese sausage (lop cheong), chopped
- 3   large fresh shrimp, peeled, deveined, and cut
  in half lengthwise
- 6   pieces squid (fresh or frozen)
- ¼   teaspoon salt
- 1   teaspoon oyster sauce
- 1   teaspoon sambal oelek (Indonesian red chile paste)
- ½   teaspoon dark soy sauce

Chopped chives and green onion
Sesame seeds

Ingredient notes

- If you don't live near a Chinese noodle factory, order dried wide rice noodles online or use fettuccine.
- Instead of Chinese sausage (a sweetish, air-dried pork sausage flavored with 5-spice powder), brown a half-pound ground pork with a little soy sauce and 5-spice powder.
- And if you don't like squid, double the shrimp.

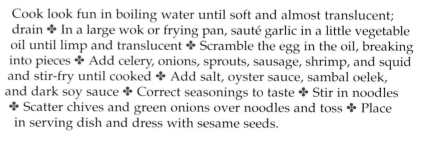

Cook look fun in boiling water until soft and almost translucent; drain ❖ In a large wok or frying pan, sauté garlic in a little vegetable oil until limp and translucent ❖ Scramble the egg in the oil, breaking into pieces ❖ Add celery, onions, sprouts, sausage, shrimp, and squid and stir-fry until cooked ❖ Add salt, oyster sauce, sambal oelek, and dark soy sauce ❖ Correct seasonings to taste ❖ Stir in noodles ❖ Scatter chives and green onions over noodles and toss ❖ Place in serving dish and dress with sesame seeds.

❖ *Serves 2.*

Among the elusive recipes readers request often is Lemon Crunch Cake, a chiffon tube cake frosted with a whipped cream studded with piquant lemon candy, a specialty of the Alexander Young Hotel bakery. That hotel, which opened in downtown Honolulu in 1901 and was demolished, to Islanders' dismay, in 1981, was famed alike for its reasonably priced hotel rooms, rooftop tea dances, and exceptional baked goods. Alas! Those recipes disappeared as surely as did the building at Bishop and Hotel Streets. This is as close as we can get, based on one published in the San Francisco Chronicle in 1999.

Company Lemon Crunch Cake | Appeared Aug. 4, 1999

- 6 eggs, separated
- 1/2 cup cold water
- 1 1/2 cups sugar
- 1/2 teaspoon vanilla extract
- 1/3 teaspoon lemon extract

- 1 1/2 cups flour
- 1/4 teaspoon salt
- 3/4 teaspoon cream of tartar
- Frosting (recipe follows)

Preheat oven to 325 degrees ❖ Beat egg yolks until thick and lemon-colored ❖ Add water and continue to beat until thick ❖ Gradually add sugar, vanilla, and lemon extract ❖ Sift together flour and salt and fold into mixture in 4 additions ❖ With an electric mixer, beat the egg whites in a large bowl until foamy; add cream of tartar and beat until stiff peaks form to form meringue ❖ Gently fold meringue into batter using an up-and-under motion, not stirring ❖ Turn into an ungreased 10-inch angel food cake pan ❖ Bake for 1 hour ❖ Cool upside down on wire rack; allow to cool for a while before attempting to remove from pan.

❖ *Serves 8 to 10.*

Lemon Frosting:

- 1 1/2 cups plus 2 tablespoons sugar
- 1/3 cup water
- 1/4 cup corn syrup
- 1 tablespoon baking soda
- 1/8 teaspoon oil of lemon or lemon extract or 2 teaspoons grated lemon zest

- 2 cups whipping cream
- 2 tablespoons sour cream
- 1 tablespoon lemon extract

> ## "The new Alexander Young Hotel Roof Garden is open!"
> — *Jan. 4, 1935*

In a heavy saucepan, combine 1½ cups sugar, water, and corn syrup and bring to a boil over medium-high heat, stirring until temperature reaches 300 degrees on a candy thermometer ❖ Remove from heat ❖ Add baking soda and oil of lemon or lemon extract or grated lemon zest ❖ Pour onto an ungreased cookie sheet ❖ Do not stir or spread out ❖ Allow to cool ❖ Once it's cooled, break up lemon candy using a rolling pin; store in airtight container overnight, if desired ❖ In an electric mixer, whip whipping cream to soft peaks; whip in sour cream, 2 tablespoons sugar, and 1 teaspoon lemon extract ❖ Frost cake and dust with broken lemon candy.

About the Author

Wanda Adams is a *"Keiki o Kepaniwai,"* born and primarily raised along the Kepaniwai River in misty 'Iao Valley on Maui.

She learned to love newspapers from her grandfather, the late Sen. John Gomes Duarte, a printer for the Maui News. She got the gift of gab from her father, the late Rep. Ray Francis Adams, and her organizational skills from her mother, Adelaide Duarte Adams Rowland. And she served her culinary apprenticeship under her grandmother, Ida Sylva Duarte, who taught her to keep a pot of parsley on the back porch, fresh vegetables in the garden and something always bubbling on the stove.

She is an alumnus of the St. Anthony Schools and graduated from Lahainaluna High School in 1969. After receiving degrees in journalism and English literature from the University of Washington in 1973, she worked as a feature writer for the Everett (Washington) Herald and the Seattle Post-Intelligencer, where she was an award-winning food editor.

Desperate for a plate lunch, Adams returned to Hawai'i in 1989 as features editor of The Honolulu Advertiser. While she managed an ever-expanding staff and multiple newspaper sections, she researched Portuguese food in Hawai'i, began the Great (unfinished) Portuguese American Novel, and watched the Island food scene change.

In 2001, Adams returned to her first love— writing. As assistant features editor for food, books and travel, she enjoys covering "all the good things in life." Her Food for Thought column helps readers locate long-lost recipes and solve everyday food problems.

Adams is married to her high school sweetheart, Carl E. " Sonny" Koonce III. Between them, they have five birth, step- and hānai children. They live with their cats, Precious and Pōpoki, in Kapālama, O'ahu.